SLIDING PAST THE SHADOWS OF CATASTROPHE

THE PLACE TO START:
A 21ST CENTURY ESSAY ON IDENTITY AND SURVIVAL

RONALD D. MEANS PH.D.

outskirts
press

TABLE OF CONTENTS

Author's Preface

The global future is unfolding as it always has in the midst of infinite complexities; but today these seem more forbidding than before, more wrapped up together, more difficult to disentangle and address. Now, as always, humanity is confronted by the perennial existential question of what to do in these particular times and circumstances? What to do to face up to and address this century's challenges: climate change and its accumulating fallouts, the darkening possibilities of nuclear devastations, the undermining of the life supporting environment, the risks of uncontrollable pandemics, of massive displacements of populations, of genocidal conflicts, of economic overreach and collapse, of tyrannical restrictions on freedom, thought, and constructive creativity. What is to be done to understand and cope with the unprecedented transformational impacts of the digital revolution, genetic science, android medicine, and robotics? What is to be done to mitigate hatreds, to encourage healing collaborations, to overcome the self-centered divisive ignorance shared to some extent by every human being and to build the moral order on which all hope depends?

If humankind is to survive in a civilized global society it must find its way to constructive responses. Taken together the challenges when clearly recognized are so overpowering, so spirit crushing, so demoralizing, that they beg avoidance. But they must be addressed if humankind is to slide past the looming shadows of catastrophe. If it is to reach a better place, it must wake up, peer ahead, analyze the threats, and with prudent foresight take evasive action. It cannot afford to drift beneath the shadows, reacting with much too little much too late. Neglect of the challenges each by each raises the odds that they will eventually come together, dramatically coalesce, and strike a catastrophic blow at the human prospect.

Neither I nor anyone else will be able to present a persuasively detailed plan for coping with an unpredictable, infinitely complex, future. But it is possible to start with a plausible answer to the most basic question. What can each of us do as severely limited human beings, whatever our circumstances, whatever our locations in time and space, whatever our political, religious, cultural, and intellectual life-worlds, whatever our nationalities, whatever our racial and ethnic backgrounds, to face up to the existential challenges confronting humankind and contribute in whatever small ways we can to coping with them constructively?

I propose an answer to this question which is simple enough and understandable enough to offer comprehensible guidance to individuals, whether they belong to highly educated elites or are quite ordinary people of modest educational attainments, which offers each and all a starting place, a direction for self-development, and a platform on which to stand for coping with the challenges to their life-worlds, immediate and long range. I call this starting place, this pathway to self-development, the morality of the mind, imagination and engagement. To offer guidance for engaging with the existential challenges, I condense an open-ended list of possibilities into two overarching interrelated long-term goals. The morality imposes the obligation to commit oneself to truth-seeking rooted in the evidence, however difficult and uncertain that may be, to nurturing curiosity, to endorsing and appreciating the creativity lying behind humankind's most useful and valuable achievements, to cultivating an imaginative and empathetic understanding of others and their life-worlds, and to engaging in the promotion of these values.

This morality is welded to the two interconnected goals which give direction, focus, and guidance to the project. The first goal is to relentlessly pursue the realization of the common, to discover and work towards those commonalities which bind humankind together, which are foundational to the global village. The second goal is to minimize waste, particularly the wastage of the global environment and of healthy and meaningful lives for those millions of human beings who are left behind among the wasted.

My proposal rests on two debatable assumptions. I assume that what has long been referred to as human nature is so deeply and stubbornly rooted in humankind that it will remain essentially unchanged throughout the decades ahead. This is both encouraging and frightening. I also assume that in spite of all the chasms which continue to divide, that humankind is becoming a singularity, that this broad-brush abstraction keeps gathering meaning, because the fate of every human being is becoming ever more dependent on the fate of every other, and that virtually everywhere the local is being transformed into the global. Individuals concerned with the shape of the future must begin to think, as difficult as that may be, from the perspectives of this emerging singularity; which means they must ultimately direct their thinking towards the global and the general welfare of humankind.

Beneath this singularity, the challenges are formidable. Beyond the imperative of survival in a human world endangered by existential threats, what does every human being have in common with every other beyond belonging to the same species, beyond what everyone shares as a psycho-biological product of evolution? Each individual exists in a particular life-world which is unique in the sense that is distinct from every other. Each individual life-world acquires its content and meaning from the wider life-worlds of family, society, and culture, and these life-worlds are of limitless variety. It is the aim of the Place to Start to respond to these ineradicable human differences by offering attractive pathways to discovering and acting on those commonalities essential to a viable and humane global civilization. As idealistic and naive as this may seem, it must be tried.

My proposal of a place to start is divided into two closely related sections, each reflecting my own identity as the author. Part I, A Global Project for the 21st Century, reflects my self-identification as a citizen of the global village. Part II, As Americans What Must We Do? reflects my identity as a patriotic citizen. These two parts represent my attempt to reconcile and integrate these identities. Others attracted to the project may find a similar need to reconcile and integrate parallel identities. We live in nations. We live in a world. We must accommodate our identities to both.

Part I, A Global Project for the 21st Century is "global" because the most forbidding existential challenges are global. It is a "project" because it opens pathways to plausible responses. It is "for the 21st Century" because no short-term undertakings will ultimately suffice. It is an invitation to individuals to participate in "the morality" and "the goals" to encourage their self-development in the directions of freedom and understanding, and to focus their commitment on whatever contributions it may be possible for them to make in the struggle to shape a better future.

In Part II, As Americans What Must We Do? I attack the political, economic, and cultural sicknesses which are afflicting my country, weakening its institutions, and undermining its leadership in the world. I argue that the United States must put its house in order and recognize that global leadership throughout the years ahead will depend less on an economic and military predominance which is being neutralized by others than by presenting a persuasive example to the world of a healthy flourishing democratic society and, most critically, by moving out in front of others, by seizing the lead in developing global responses to the existential challenges of the 21st Century. If the United States fails to respond to these challenges, wisely and aggressively, then others may confront them by imposing authoritarian solutions, by embedding division and hatred more deeply than ever in the human story.

President Trump has made the recovery of a healthy democratic political culture more difficult by ignoring and subverting traditional and constitutional norms. As a result, the United States has taken a step closer to the end of the American Republic, to the demise of a flourishing and mature democratic polity, towards a political façade covering hallowed out institutions and a cynically managed electorate. Not only must the United States cope with all the other looming shadows of catastrophe but with this undermining danger to its essence.

A global movement which starts with the project's morality and aspires towards its goals may be mandatory if the existential challenges of the 21st Century are to be successfully confronted. Many gifted people in the United States and across the world may need to take up this cause, find each other, and work towards building a movement of unprecedented transformational power. As impractical as this may seem, its practicality may emerge as the most worrisome challenges of the 21st Century close in. Unfortunately, its pertinence may only become obvious from underneath the looming shadows of catastrophe.

Sliding Past the Shadows of Catastrophe is neither a research project nor an academic paper and is presented without a bibliography.

This should not be taken to mean that I haven't recognized my debt to others. I have drawn upon an immense open-ended bibliography of books, articles, and people; on a lifetime of reading; on my education at Michigan State, Harvard, and Cornell; on teaching history and government in a public high school and the humanities in university classrooms; and on many rewarding years as the Executive Director of the Michigan Humanities Council and in that role as an advocate for the place of the humanities in American life. My essay is my own take on what I've learned and on what is happening in the world around me. My purpose is to attract others, not necessarily to agree on particulars, but to take a similar approach in facing up to what must be done.

Ronald D. Means Ph.D.

PART I
A GLOBAL PROJECT FOR THE 21ST CENTURY

AN INTRODUCTION

A Global Project for the 21st Century contends that humankind will have its best chance to achieve a socially and materially viable world if it pursues two overarching goals within a framework of values called the morality of mind, imagination, and engagement. These goals are the minimization of waste, the wastage of human beings and of the life supporting conditions upon which humankind depends; and a fresh understanding of the common, of shared commonalities and of how these may come to be embedded in social and cultural values, and in political and economic arrangements. Taken together these moral values combined with these overarching goals opens up promising pathways for achieving a peaceful and humane global society by the end of the 21st Century.

The project depends on the commitments of individual human beings for whom the fact of existence precedes who they may become as conscious thinking and acting persons. Everyone is dependent on genetic makeup, is shaped by human nurture or a lack of it, by surrounding material and cultural realities, and by innumerable impactful contingencies; but a commitment to self-development allows room for individual choices which enhance understanding, focus energies, and help shape personhood. The project is to be understood as an invitation to make these choices within a particular intellectual and moral framework and in pursuit of two overarching goals. It invites individuals into a meaningful and constructive approach to their life- worlds.

In spite of its pretentious title A Global Project for the 21st Century is critically self-limiting. It does not predict the future. It rejects the prevailing ideologies as short-sighted and misleading. It is not a religion, but it understands that spiritual experiences should never be arbitrarily dismissed as mere psychological phenomena because they have a way of arising at the very center of humankind's search for meaning. It is not strictly speaking a philosophy, though it touches on the origins of philosophical thinking and has an implicit connection to existentialism.

The global challenges to the human future are daunting and inter-related. The deeply worrisome impacts of climate change add dire potentialities to virtually every other challenge. Environmental degradation continues. Shortages of food and fresh water may reach catastrophic levels. The world is beset by ideological, ethnic, religious, and international tensions which may deteriorate into life destroying conflicts. Population growth increases all the pressures. The seemingly unlikely but not inconceivable possibility of nuclear war remains an existential hazard. Shortfalls in humane and effective governance are a widespread global problem. Corruption weakens and undermines essential institutions. Prosperity may hide distortions and fragilities in the economic system which may take hold as nasty destabilizing surprises.

Populations are on the move or locked away in refugee camps or urban slums-- destitute, bitter, and potentially ungovernable. The dangerous abyss between rich and poor widens. The global middle class is insecure and troubled. The digital revolution gathers momentum and spreads its amazing benefits; but it may lead to permanent joblessness even among the highly qualified. It is revolutionizing communications with positive and negative impacts which have yet to be sorted out. This long list of challenges isn't all-inclusive; nor is it possible to anticipate grave challenges which surely will arise. Life-extinguishing dystopian fantasies claim a highly visible and entertaining place in popular culture. But the underlying possibilities are real.

The project is not to be mistaken for a utopian vision or misperceived as a political and economic blueprint for the future. It is not a scheme for governing the world. It is first and foremost an invitation to individual human beings to adopt a particular life-stance, a particular perspective on the world, to foster an identity of self from which to proceed in whatever ways their life commitments allow to help shape a viable future for humankind, an empowering perspective from which to work through the infinite array of obstacles, large and small, which stand in the way of the global future.

The project is profoundly conservative. It assumes that human beings will remain who and what they are through the decades ahead, that they will not undergo biologic/genetic or robotic transformations which will make them remarkably different beings than they are today. This assumption does not imply opposition to continuing progress in understanding, preventing, and treating diseases or in helping individuals overcome their limitations. Everyone should hope for many lifesaving and life-enhancing advances in the years ahead. The project is also conservative, even radically conservative as things now stand, in its advocacy of living constructively within a cluster of interrelated values rooted in the past, values which lie behind not only the most creative and valuable achievements of humankind, but which remain an everyday necessity in a civilized society.

The project presents a pathway for distancing oneself from political, economic and cultural realities, from everything about them which is distorting, shallow, and manipulative. Out of this detached perspective an imperative arises to investigate, to reflect upon, and to engage with these realities while keeping in mind the goals of realizing the meaning of the common and of minimizing waste. For those committed to the project this distancing, this imperative towards understanding, these engagements guided by overarching goals, may blend together as habits of the mind, imagination, and engagement.

THE PLACE TO START

Chapter 1

THE MORALITY OF MIND, IMAGINATION, AND ENGAGEMENT

THIS MORALITY COULD be called an "ethic", but "morality" is better. As an old-fashioned more categorically demanding word than "ethic", "morality" implies those subjective commitments to standards of behavior which are often referred to as "the conscience." This morality must be internalized if it is to become an empowering source of personal guidance. Nevertheless, it is not a system of authoritarian commands; nor does it supersede traditional moral codes. It is not a substitute for religious and ethical traditions which support loving kindness and constructive social behavior. It is a cluster of values which, in their necessary and dynamic inter-relationships give to the use of the word "morality" both its legitimacy and its force.

Each of the moral categories, mind, imagination, and engagement, is a broadly inclusive concept which doesn't need to be sharply defined. They flow together and are experienced more of less seamlessly. All three assume consciousness at work, a consciousness which freely experiences itself as thinking, as reflecting, as meditating, as analyzing, as imagining, as creating, as choosing, as initiating action, all without regard to whatever bio-psychological or philosophical arguments could be advanced against free will. This freedom in consciousness is available to virtually everyone, but in many human beings it is sadly attenuated or hideously distorted or virtually lost in imprisonments of the self. An underlying purpose of this proposal is to encourage all of humankind to discover and cultivate this internal freedom as the most fundamental freedom of them all. It is an invitation to a mature identity which is holistic, outreaching, and unselfish.

To understand the morality of mind, imagination, and engagement it is necessary to consider its essential features. These may be called "categories", but because they are so intertwined in the activities of consciousness, calling them "features" may eliminate the impression that they are rigidly divided.

TRUTH-SEEKING

At the center of the morality of the mind is the search for truth, for seeking truth with the humble recognition that what appears to be true today may have to be reviewed tomorrow in light of fresh evidence and insight. But it rejects the contention that there is no truth to be found or that all truth is merely relative, positions which may be unnecessarily cynical and or simply self-serving.(Note #1) Truth-seeking requires respect for evidence, carefully assessed, and for those scientists, scholars, and journalists who scrupulously uphold the truth-seeking standards of their fields; and for the sincere efforts of all other truth seekers, however sophisticated or untutored.

The morality of mind, imagination, and engagement is not, nor can it be, exclusively for persons belonging to elites. To have a meaningful impact on the 21st Century it must be widely participated in, virtually

    SLIDING PAST THE SHADOWS OF CATASTROPHE

universalized as a moral obligation. Every person should have, as an inalienable right, opportunities to cultivate their curiosity and participate in meaningful searches for what is true. Education and public policy should support this. But the morality lies in the search, not necessarily in the results. People arrive at different and contradictory truths. Each mind is a reality filtering universe unto itself. Each is confronted by externalities which are often ruthlessly ambiguous and obscure. Respect for the facts does not mean that it is easy to determine and distinguish what are and what are not the facts. The moral force lies in the seriousness and honesty of the truth-seeking. If truth is to be found at all, it must begin with that. Common sense may sometimes bring truth closer than intellectual analysis.

This moral commitment to truth-seeking implies distaste for prevarications and may lead to a deeply felt aversion to lying, particularly to those big self-serving politically, economically, and ideologically motivated lies which are used to manipulate human beings and which may be considered, figuratively speaking, as mortal sins against the morality of mind, imagination, and engagement.

IMAGINING

Imagining is an activity of consciousness distanced from immediate sense perceptions, an internal generation of dreams, of images, of insights and ideas, of everything real and unreal in a life-world. Virtually unlimited in wherever it may turn it may or it may not have anything to do with the morality of the imagination. That morality depends on its relationships to curiosity and the search for truth. It generates an opening to the world, a reaching out from one's life-world into the life-worlds of others, a reaching out enlarged and enriched by the mind's and imagination's explorations of the realities in which human beings live their lives, not only their personal situations, but the political, economic, and social circumstances, the histories, the religions, and the cultures.

This imaginative effort at understanding does not imply approval; to understand is not necessarily to forgive. But to look closely at the biographies of, say, Adolf Hitler and Joseph Stalin, and at the historical circumstances, and the pernicious ideologies, through which they arose to become world-shaking manifestations of evil is to consider cautionary tales for anyone who hopes to cope constructively with the political, economic and social upheavals which may lie ahead. Bettering the lot of humankind and mitigating evil rest, in large measure, on an imaginative, empathetic, and critical grasp of individuals and their circumstances.

CURIOSITY

Curiosity is the impulse which drives the morality of mind, imagination, and engagement. It begins in a passion to imagine, to see into things, to understand, and to learn. This admirable tendency is most common in children. Although it may not be as spontaneously natural in most adults, it may be cultivated by reaching out beyond the familiar towards the new; by looking deeply into the life-worlds of others; by asking thoughtful questions; and by examining personal assumptions and strongly held beliefs; by reflecting on life's discoveries and surprises; and by being open to whatever fresh perspectives may emerge from these investigations. Cultivating curiosity can be difficult and unsettling. But it is the road to maturity and growth, and to employ another old-fashioned word to wisdom. Once this is said, it must be acknowledged that outside the moral framework of mind, imagination, and engagement curiosity can open the way to the deeply troubling, to behavior which is destructive to the self and to others.

CREATIVITY

Creativity is the power of mind and imagination to come up with fresh and often surprising combinations of ideas. Without creativity

    SLIDING PAST THE SHADOWS OF CATASTROPHE

humankind would not have developed stone tools, founded complex societies, generated scientific, technological, and industrial revolutions, and produced great works of philosophy, literature, history, and the arts. Without creativity, on the other hand, humankind could not have devised all those imaginative and diabolical means it uses to kill, torture, enslave and oppress one another. The morality of mind, imagination, and engagement supports creativity in directions which are consistent with its other values. It supports and is nurtured by the authentic creations of artists, musicians, writers, and others which lift the spirits of humankind and open windows into the human story, into its richness, into its plights and potentialities, into suffering and joy.

Creativity is not only a formative power in the human story, but it is hidden in the most mundane realities of daily life. The repetitive mechanisms of habit are not sufficient in themselves for human beings to navigate their life-worlds. Fresh combinations of information are continuously required in order to maneuver successfully through daily life. The success of the Global Project depends on creativity, on fresh ideas and on the discovery of creative ways, however mundane, to support the goals of minimizing waste and the realization of a humane society expressive of the common.

Living creatures live only in the present. Humankind draws upon the past to engage with a future which isn't reliably predictable however persuasive the current trends, however captivating the visions of the futurists. The likelihood that what is foreseen will actually occur tends to diminish over time. This is a severe limitation on utopian plans for building a new world in the distant future. To focus ideas and energy on achieving a predetermined vision of this world is to pursue a mirage across deserts of uncertainty. This does not mean, however, that the two fundamental goals for achieving the well-being of humankind, the realization of the common and the minimization of waste, cannot be pursued independent of visionary formulations of the future. If pursued with determination in the present the most plausible visions of a better future may eventually emerge.

There are thoughtful people throughout the world who are personally curious, who place a high value on truth-seeking, whose imaginations are open to empathetic understandings, and who are engaged constructively in the world around them. Not only are these people to be found among principled scientists, scholars, writers, journalists, jurists, and artists, but among innumerable others, those parents and teachers, for example, who encourage curiosity, truth telling, a respect for facts, mutual understanding, critical thinking, the cultivation of the imagination through stories, and creativity through arts and crafts. If they were to join together and support these moral values and focus them on the 21st Century goals of minimizing waste and the realization of the common, then the Global Project might eventually succeed in creating a stable, peaceful, world.

The morality of mind, imagination, and engagement does not reside within a group, however supportive a particular group may be, whatever powers of influence or enforcement a group may have. It resides in individuals. That's where it begins and that is where it remains no matter how an individual may absorb it, live by it, and collaborate with others in promoting and applying it.

The morality of mind, imagination, and engagement is dependent on the holistic identities of individuals, and on its predominant place in their conscious activities. Personal identities are extraordinarily complex. Each person is a unique island of consciousness. This is no less true even though there are many aspects of personal identity which are widely shared and subject to a boundless array of meanings and interpretations; among these are gender, race, language and ethnicity, religious and secular beliefs, social class, family and tribal ties, degrees of poverty and wealth. Each of these may or may not be pertinent to how a particular individual relates to the morality of mind, imagination, and engagement. The Global Project is highly individualistic in its commitment to the morality of mind, imagination, and engagement; but it is also highly social in its commitment to the realization of the common and the minimization waste.

Internalizing Freedom

The morality of mind, imagination, and engagement as a central pathway to the development of the self is to submit to freedom which is internal and which if it is to be strengthened and maintained carries within itself the stark necessity of courage. It is cowardly, for instance, to fail to admit to oneself what is perceived to be true because what is perceived to be true is too dangerous or runs contrary to one's interests or assumptions. Engagement, the externalizing directive, should be supported by perceptions of what is true and an imaginative awareness of possibilities.

In the liberal democracies, the laws and the judicial systems are intended to protect the basic freedoms of the individual and to restrain the individual from exercising freedom in ways destructive to others and to the society's principal institutions. This is the social contract within which the individual is expected to behave. In oppressive societies, these basic freedoms are suppressed and their exercise may be harshly punished by torture, imprisonment, and death.

In the United States freedom is understood as the right to be yourself, to think for yourself, and to make your own choices. This is perfectly consistent with the morality of mind, imagination, and engagement. But there is this profound difference. In the morality of mind, imagination, and engagement freedom is internalized, and independent of an external context, while in the United States, freedom is widely perceived in its relationships to certain externalities, particularly rights of free speech and assembly, and all other rights protected by the Constitution of the United States.

In American culture, free market capitalism has come to occupy a predominant place. It encompasses such widely supported expectations as the right to start a business or to choose or change an occupation and to be rewarded for hard work and entrepreneurial initiative. None of this is necessarily inconsistent with the morality of mind, imagination, and engagement. But this doesn't mean that it is consistent with those moral values to regard economic freedom as a predominant absolute, as though it were so basic among the freedoms that it must not be regulated and channeled to serve the public interest. Treating economic freedom as an absolute, challenges the morality of the mind, imagination, and engagement, and the prospect of achieving the project's overarching goals.

The culture of economic freedom energizes a capitalist economic system which is a great creative achievement of humankind. Today it is a powerful driver of change in a globalizing civilization. Through its alliance with science and technology it grows consumption-based societies in which, given the choice, most of humankind would prefer to live. But it can also seriously undermine the morality, of mind, imagination, and engagement; erect formidable barriers to the realization of the common; and, sometimes to an obscene degree contribute to the wastage of the global environment and of human life.

Before I proceed to elaborate on these matters further down in this proposal, I must insist that I do not intend a blanket rejection of the capitalist system or the demonization of the hard-working, constructive, and creative individuals who are making this enormously complex system function with considerable success. This proposal is not a left-wing attack on capitalism. Capitalism like most of humankind's major institutional creations is riddled with contradictions which must

     SLIDING PAST THE SHADOWS OF CATASTROPHE

be worked through or around. But capitalism in its all-encompassing nature presents formidable obstacles to the success of the 21ˢᵗ Century Project, to its moral values and its goals.

Recognition of the Spiritual

Experiences understood as spiritual occupy a permanent place in the story of humankind. They stand behind and sustain religious institutions and cultures and are of critical importance in the lives of many who are not participants in a religion, who live on the secular side of the divide, but have personal experiences which they interpret as spiritual.

These experiences do not prove the existence of God. That perennial battle may be left to the theists and the atheists. Today both sides are defending their positions with arguments drawn from their interpretations of science. Setting that perennial debate aside, these experiences must be taken seriously. Those committed to the Global Project must acknowledge their significance as they navigate their way towards the realization of the common.

Spiritual experiences in their great variety are hard to definitively pin down. They may range from an awe-inspiring awareness of a star-filled sky, to an intimate closeness to God in prayer, to uplifting romantic love, to the loss of self in the divine whatever religious disciplines or chemical ingredients may pave the way to this mystic state, to an overwhelming experience of aesthetic satisfaction when an architectural or artistic vision is achieved. Most important to the project is an awareness and readiness to respond to the transformative power which spiritual experiences often have. They can change a person's sense of self, their understanding of the externalities surrounding them, their behavior, and their goals. When Christians claim salvation through Jesus Christ, they may be doing no more than sincerely expressing a religious belief or they may have gone through a spiritual experience which has transformed their lives, making them experience themselves as new and better people.

When it comes to this transformative power, there are no religious or cultural monopolies. Frequently, they have been preceded by deep depressions, which in the western tradition have been referred to as "dark nights of the soul." They have been at the biographic center of the lives of transformational personalities: founders of religions, of philosophies, and of revolutionary movements; of charismatic men and women who have attracted converts and created significant institutions. Typically, these personalities have understood and expressed their experiences according to the time, the place, and the linguistic and cultural universe in which they happened to be living. Whether one interprets this powerful theme in the story of humankind as mystical or as psychological or as belonging to some plausible synthesis of the two, it must be taken seriously. It may become the source of historical surprises which could challenge or give support to the goals of 21st Century Project.

PATHWAYS TO KNOWLEDGE

Humankind has created pathways to knowledge and understanding which reach far beyond the truth and wisdom any individual could hope to acquire. The standard short list of these includes the sciences, the social sciences, the humanities, and the arts. Mathematics and technology must be included in this list. These creations and discoveries of humankind have led the way to the world we live in. The search for knowledge and understanding is a hugely complicated enterprise which can be broken down into long evolving lists of specialties and subspecialties. To become truly competent in one of these may require exceptional aptitudes and a commitment of years.

Science is our most reliable source for objective truth. As a human enterprise, it has had its own bitter internal feuds. It is the target of politically and religiously motivated attacks. Think of those who deny the human contribution to climate change. Think of those who deny biological evolution. Think of all those anti-intellectuals, whatever their motives, who fail to recognize the difference between "theory" and scientifically established fact. It is not that science never makes mistakes or that scientists never cheat by fabricating their results. But science moves forward by working its way around dead ends and past its mistakes towards correct conclusions. At its core science is a self-correcting truth-seeking enterprise and consequently has a central place in the morality of mind, imagination, and engagement.

Through history, philosophy, literature, and the arts the humanities are essential to understanding the story of humankind. They represent an indispensable source for learning who we have been and who we have become, and for understanding the intellectual and imaginative achievements of humankind. The Global Project depends upon the truism that the best chance of dealing humanely and constructively with the present and the future rests upon an enlightened and seriously cultivated understanding of the past.

The social sciences occupy an evolving middle ground between science and the humanities. Without attempting an exhaustive list, they include sociology, political science, economics, anthropology, psychology, and linguistics. They are essential sources for theoretical, statistically based, and analytical understandings of human behavior.

There is considerable artificiality in the distinctions among these various pathways towards truth. The mind and imagination are not rigidly organized by intellectual disciplines and academic departments. To use a favored term from academia itself, the mind and imagination are much more interdisciplinary than that. In reflecting upon and engaging with all the externalities the mind and imagination must draw upon whatever sources of guidance are perceived to be most helpful in the search for truth and understanding.

Worrisome issues often call for solutions which are neither simple nor clear cut. These issues often have the best chance of being dealt with satisfactorily if assessed within a rich interdisciplinary context which includes not only the pertinent facts and the applicable scientific and technical knowledge, but insights drawn from the humanities and the social sciences. It may be helpful, for instance, to acquire an historical understanding of the origins of a problem and of how similar problems have been dealt with in the past. It may be helpful to have a rich understanding of relevant social, cultural, and economic conditions and trends and, if the search for a solution is controversial, an awareness of the motivations of opposing parties. It may be helpful for clarity of understanding if the worrisome issue is analytically disaggregated into its constituent parts and each is thoroughly investigated.

This approach is the gold standard for the successful resolution of complex issues. It is obviously impractical for most everyday decision making, but to understand it may have a useful influence on habits of thought, and it should be turned to for comprehending and resolving the controversial issues of the times. This gold standard needs to be seriously and judiciously applied if the trajectory of the 21st Century is to be towards the eventual achievement of the project's goals.

The relationship between the project's morality and goals and "ideology" needs to be explained. Loosely defined, "ideology" may be taken to mean the set of attitudes, assumptions, and beliefs of each and every human being. In this sense, the global project may be taken as an attempt to persuade individuals to adopt a particular ideology. But the word, "ideology" is often used in a more restrictive sense.

     SLIDING PAST THE SHADOWS OF CATASTROPHE

It is applied within the public domain to controversial systems of ideas, political, economic, or social. It has a central place in various partisanships. Typically, these ideologies adhere, more or less rigidly, to ideas which may or may not be systematically related, which in significant respects may be internally contradictory, and which tend to override plausible alternatives whatever arguments and evidence may be presented in their support. These ideologies are always too simplistic for the real world, for comprehending and dealing with its infinite complexities. They stand in the way of the creative openness which is so often necessary for dealing effectively with the emerging and the new.

The morality of mind, imagination, and engagement is not an ideology in this more restrictive sense, though it carries within itself an implied relationship to every ideology, a moral relationship which is pre-ideological in its values and perspectives. It evaluates the ideas of the ideologue and the evidence with which these ideas are supported as it would any other ideas, or any other body of evidence. If the ideologue is advocating evidence-based ideas which could, for example, contribute to the minimization of waste, then that position could be supported or even fought for as consistent with those values which make it possible to stand outside that ideology on a pre-ideological platform. It encourages, whenever possible, the laying aside of ideological and other intellectual rigidities for open forthright discussions, and when consensus cannot be reached, then a mutually acceptable compromise, and, when that is impossible, not war, but a civilized truce.

Beliefs and ideologies obviously overlap. Ideological systems emerge from and are supported by firmly held beliefs. Ideologues, especially passionately committed ideologues, believe absolutely in their systems. The Global Project is not an attack on beliefs, secular or religious, but encourages believers to participate in the morality, of mind, imagination, and engagement and to support the project's overarching goals to whatever extent they can. To do so, it may help them enrich their own traditions and connect more realistically to contemporary challenges. The Global Project encourages them to take intellectual and imaginative risks for the sake of greater openness to the life-worlds of others and for a more promising future for themselves.

Philosophers and theologians have created and continue to create comprehensive systems of ideas which are intended to provide intellectually consistent world views rooted in what they understand to be the evidence. Behind each of these systems lies the search for truth, a motivating curiosity about the nature of reality, an imaginative capacity to create intellectual structures, and an effort to understand human nature and the implications of the human predicament. These systems vary tremendously. They are imaginative products of individual life-worlds by brilliant human beings nurtured and surrounded by the culture of their time and place. Among the most influential in the intellectual history of the West are Plato and Aristotle; Augustine and Aquinas; Luther and Calvin; Rousseau and Locke; Descartes, Kant, Hegel, and Marx; Galileo, Newton, Darwin, Freud, and Einstein; and skipping to today, the French theorists, Foucault, Deleuze, Derrida and others, who, though their influence has faded in France, dominate critical thinking and teaching in many American humanities departments, which makes them particularly relevant to an essay in which the humanities have an essential place.

This domination of humanities departments by French theory can be explained in ways which are not mutually exclusive. It can be understood as a defensive reaction to the relentless marginalization of the humanities in American culture and to the dwindling role of the humanities in higher education, and to the perception, particularly among the affected academics, that the humanities are under siege. It must also be understood as an empathetic effort to help students cope

    SLIDING PAST THE SHADOWS OF CATASTROPHE

critically and imaginatively with the oppressive conditions, political, economic, and cultural, which are impinging on their lives and undermining their confidence in the future. Finally, this devotion to French theory must also be understood as a commitment to a brilliant intellectual culture which can seem spectacularly relevant, which is loaded with insights and ideas, and which is continually renewing itself in critical fine-tuned arguments worthy of the medieval scholastics. This intellectual milieu deserves, if not awe, at least respect, even if one is not fully drawn to it. Like other serious philosophical attempts at comprehensive understanding, French theory begins, a priori, in the morality of mind, imagination, and engagement.

In respect to human happiness, to becoming fully oneself, for freely exercising personality, for allowing room for a sense of humor, and for an eclectic appreciation of the arts, the morality of mind, imagination and engagement is more open than many ideologies. The intellectual and imaginative self-limitations of an ideology can distort perspective, imprison personality, feed distrust and hatred, and inhibit the spontaneity that contributes so much to happiness. The morality of mind, imagination, and engagement offers a pathway to self-development which rejects ideological self-imprisonment for openness and freedom, and it may be added, a position from which to laugh at absurdity and nonsense.

The assertions in this proposal of the moral imperatives of mind, imagination and engagement may be dismissed by the intellectually offended as warmed-over Enlightenment philosophy seasoned by a forced attempt to put morality behind it. Up to a point this dismissive tie to the Enlightenment is plausible. The values of curiosity, of rationality, of evidence-based quests for truth, of hostility to oppression and oppressors, and to lies and liars, all belong inside the cornerstone of the Enlightenment. But, the morality of mind, imagination, and engagement is significantly more inclusive than the more superficial understandings of the Enlightenment. As the Place to Start, it is an ideology for our times, a synthesis of values from which to assess every other ideology.

Chapter 2

THE OVERARCHING GOALS

THE FIRST GOAL is to arrive at fresh understandings of the common, of shared commonalities and of how these may come to be embedded in social and cultural values, and in political and economic arrangements. The second is to minimize waste, the wastage of human beings and of the life- supporting conditions upon which humankind depends. The project contends that these are the necessary existential guidelines for confronting both present challenges and the unpredictable happenings which will face humankind throughout the years ahead. The morality of mind, imagination, and engagement points towards them as mandatory pathways for sliding past the shadows of catastrophe.

The hope is that the necessities of survival will force humanity to close ranks and work together to find a way around the looming shadows of catastrophe and to eventually reach these overarching goals But isn't it at least as likely that humanity will become even more narrowly tribal, xenophobic, and selfish than today, that it will be prepared to let outsiders die off or even to engage in their destruction? If the boat becomes too crowded will these outsiders be tossed to the sharks? Genocide may become contagious in an overcrowded world beset by catastrophic happenings. Everything must be done to avoid that.

REALIZING THE MEANING OF THE COMMON

Ultimately, the common encompasses everything there is and its relevance to every human being is incontestable. Everyone is born into the common, on its largest scale into an all-embracing universe which confronts everyone with a message of irrelevant minuteness and inevitable death. Though humbled by this message and the surrounding cosmic vastness, humankind possesses countervailing gifts for understanding its astrophysical properties, and for ageless perceptions of its mystical suggestiveness. Without humankind, and perhaps without other similar creatures as yet unknown, the universe would be no more than an empty page.

To state the obvious, the planet earth stands today as humankind's irreplaceable commonality whatever dreams some may have of colonizing Mars, the moons of Jupiter and Saturn, and of reaching out to nearby stars. All are dependent on the earth's support of human life. This universal dependency implies that all hold the world in common however obscure this common ownership has become.

Ownership of the earth is shared by rich and poor alike. This basic fact is confronted by the conundrum of property, of who owns what and why. What ought to be kept in the public domain for the well-being of all? What should be protected as private property for various reasons, some more persuasive than others, such as every human being's need to possess some measure of personal property which belongs to them and whose ownership is not only protected but inviolable? The legal challenges of ownership, particularly of the land, the built environment, and the tools of productivity, if reasonably and fairly dealt with, can provide powerful sources of support for freedom, democracy, and social stability.

The Global Project stands back from the evolving world of philosophical and legal doctrines which offer resolutions to tensions and conflicts over property. It is not an "ism"; it is not advocating some communist or communitarian scheme. Moreover, it implies that to be even plausibly acceptable schemes which would do away with private property must include principles and methods for serving socially critical needs now protected as private property. It is impossible to know what arrangements could be worked out by the end of the 21st Century for resolving the property conundrum humanely and in the common interest. But the pursuit of the common absolutely requires the universalizing of the communitarian spirit, the recognition that all of humankind lives on this earth together and that love and sharing are far more important than naked acquisitiveness

THE MINIMIZATION OF WASTE

Waste is inexorable. It is the ultimate terminal disease. The sun, the earth, the entire universe, will eventually waste away in whimpers and prodigious bangs. Waste is becoming an existential challenge for humankind, a looming shadow of catastrophe.

Earth itself eventually evolved into an amazing response to the unconscious, often violent materiality of the universe. It brought forth life, and through the random processes of evolution it brought forth humankind into a world rich in unexploited resources and ecosystems teeming with life. But the struggle of humankind to lay claim to these opportunities has been excruciatingly difficult and dramatically ambiguous. On the one hand, it has been the story of hatred, cruelty, and heartless destructive violence; while on the other, it has been a story of courageous self-sacrifice, communal cooperation, technical innovation and cultural creativity. Unfortunately, the commonalities achieved have been embedded quite consistently in tribalism, nationalism, and imperialism.

The highest priority must be to radically reduce the wastage of a global environment upon which human survival depends. If that fails, so does all else. But beyond this is the moral imperative to enhance the quality of life for humankind, to overcome the wastage of human beings, the wastage of their lives, of their minds and imaginations, and of their untapped potential for constructive and meaningful engagement.

Hundreds of millions are imprisoned in the life-worlds of the wasted. These life-worlds exist in the most developed countries particularly among those human beings trapped by poverty, homelessness, mental problems, and soul-destroying imprisonments. They have been increasing explosively throughout much of the world in massive urban slums, in refugee containment centers, and in rural areas amidst shriveling prospects for sustaining age-old economic practices and cultural traditions. Those afflicted in these ways often become the most bitter and dangerous people in the world. Together they represent the seething underside of a global society riddled with contradictions. To ignore the wastage of alienated populations is to court disaster. If people find that they have no place, that they are shut out, that those with the power treat them as too weak and stupid to fight back, then the time to be wary has arrived. Popular uprisings can be touched off by tiny sparks, move in unpredictable directions, undermine all the complacencies, and turn the world upside down.

The realization of the common and the minimization of waste are complementary goals. Both must be pursued if a humane and viable global civilization is to be achieved. Each is vital to the progress of the other. The meaning of the common can be realized only in so far as the wastage of the planetary environment and of the lives, minds, and hearts of human beings is radically reduced. And this reduction in wastage can only be brought about through significant progress towards the realization of the global common. Both goals imply resistance to violence, its mitigation and elimination in so far as possible. Violence is their most

     SLIDING PAST THE SHADOWS OF CATASTROPHE

dangerous adversary. It feeds upon hatreds and chaos and crushes hope. As justifiable as violence may sometimes be in self-defense and in the protection of persons, property, and institutions, on its larger scale it could destroy all hope of progress towards the project's goals.

These goals are goals not policies. They do not imply that those who are engaged in their pursuit must agree on how they are to be achieved. The Global Project is not an ideology which urges adherents to fall in behind a particular menu of policies. It is absolutely certain, nevertheless, that if those who are committed are to bring about significant change, they will need to find one another, communicate with one another, talk out differences, work out strategies and tactics, and collaborate in advocating policies which they have concluded will contribute to the minimization of waste and/or the strengthening of the common.

These goals may best be worked toward patiently, objective by objective, step by step with each objective and each step perceived as applicable to the particularities of time and place; each to be assessed, each subject to continuation, redefinition, or abandonment. The project fits rather well into the management by objectives system of Peter Drucker, the most influential business theorist of the last century. It offers overarching goals which call for the ad hoc development of timely and appropriate objectives to be pursued in support of the ultimate realization of these goals. These goals are guidelines, points of reference in the background of a policy debate. They encourage the development of policy objectives which fit the present circumstances while considering long term implications and effects.

Collaborations are essential, but much of value may be accomplished by individuals acting on their own; for instance, they may draw in others by exemplify the morality of mind, imagination, and engagement in their personal lives: by what they stand for, by what they say and do. They may initiate local efforts which minimize waste and strengthen the commonalities which every community requires. The success of the project depends on small steps taken by individuals; which, if added together with small steps taken by of others, could make the future.

These long-term overarching goals may seem too idealistic and abstract to offer consistent guidance for deciding what to do, for shaping the future in promising directions. They may seem too easily overwhelmed and set aside under the pressures of critical, life and death decisions. But what are the alternatives? What other fundamental sources of universal guidance do we have? Where will we end up without these goals, without their relentless influence on the future, without their implicit discipline, without their resistance to chaotic breakdown, without their contribution to a transformation towards the better?

     SLIDING PAST THE SHADOWS OF CATASTROPHE

Chapter 3

Immoral Counterpoints

The Global Project does not offer a vision of the future. Instead, it offers the starting place for a determined quest towards a destination hidden in uncertainties. Nevertheless, it contends that the goals of minimizing waste in all its toxic forms and the realization of the common for the benefit of humankind are virtually mandatory if a flourishing world civilization is to emerge beyond the shadows of catastrophe. It contends that the morality of mind, imagination, and engagement is the place to start if humankind is to achieve these goals.

The project can be easily dismissed as hopelessly idealistic, as resting upon an unrealistic faith in human beings who will cling stubbornly to their ignorance, who are irredeemably violent, selfish, and corrupt; whose murderous and suicidal hatreds are easy to exploit; and that even those who are thoughtfully concerned by the challenges facing humankind are likely to remain too involved in the trajectories of their own lives to commit themselves to the necessary levels of engagement.

These grounds for rejection can be countered with the argument that the values embedded in the project are evident enough in humankind to offer hope. Support is to be found among the many thoughtful and constructive human beings whose approach to the world in which they find themselves is largely consistent with the morality of mind, imagination and engagement; and among those who are acting to minimize the wastage of the environment and/or the lives and hopes of other human beings; and among all those who are promoting policies and opportunities in support of the common good, who are strengthening those ties which bind human beings together in communities. These people are present everywhere and may be predominant among those professionally committed to the wellbeing of others: health care professionals and teachers, for example.

The project aspires to draw all these individuals together, to offer them a moral platform which they may find congenial and goals for the future which may make sense to them. It seeks to encourage them to come together, if only gradually over time, and in different configurations at different times and in different places, to engage in furthering the project's goals. It offers a pathway towards a humane and peaceful revolution.

If the project is to have a chance of achieving its overarching goals, it must cope with an indeterminate number of worrisome obstacles that stand in its way, many still hiding under the shadows. Among the most visible are climate change and its emerging consequences. Terrorism is extraordinarily difficult to eradicate and raises nightmarish possibilities. There is no greater danger to humankind than the unresolved risk of nuclear war. Global-wide contrasts between great wealth and poverty are starkly visible and may generate instabilities and conflicts which will make it impossible to achieve the project's goals. Among the most formidable obstacles to the human prospect are fear and violence. Fear, the subjective threat, violence, the physical threat, feed on one another.

          SLIDING PAST THE SHADOWS OF CATASTROPHE

Formidable obstacles are embedded in the geopolitical contradiction between the growing interconnectedness of humankind driven by economic globalism, digital communications, and the dissemination of cultures, and the countervailing forces expressed in resurgent tribalism, racism, and nationalism. This volatile contradictory mixture threatens the triggering of catastrophic events. Particularly discouraging, are those national and international institutions which appear to be too unimaginative, too slow moving, too backward looking, to cope effectively with these threats.

At this point the reader may need to be reminded that the project is not committed to any particular economic or political arrangements; but promotes the discovery and evolution of whatever arrangements may best support the realization of the global common and minimizing of waste. It is not indifferent to the nature of these arrangements. But it goes no further than to present moral principles and goals necessary for their achievement. It comes at them from its position of internalized freedom and judicious distancing. Its emphasis on understanding people holistically and empathetically implies that the global transformation starts with individuals where they are and will be shaped by them

The morality of mind, imagination, and engagement recognizes the existence of behavior which is contradictory and immoral. Nevertheless, its openness and fluidity distinguish it from those rigid moral codes which tend to push humankind into narrow definitions of acceptable behavior, usually reinforced by guilt and sometimes by the criminal law.

THE DESTRUCTIVE AND THE CRUEL

If mind, imagination, and engagement are stripped of their moral content they become neutral manifestations of the conscious life which may be applied in every conceivable direction: for constructive or destructive purposes, for good or evil. Mind and imagination can conceive the most diabolical plans and engage in their implementation. Torture and the tools of torture are creations of mind and imagination motivated by cruelty and free of moral restraints. Untied to moral considerations, the mind and the imagination may be applied in ways which are either indifferent to or hostile toward the minimization of waste and the realization of the common.

LIARS AND THEIR LIES

The values most central to the morality of mind, imagination and engagement are truth-seeking supported by the evidence and the honesty to face up to unpleasant truths. Against this are the immoralities of lying, of hiding evidence, of intentional distortions of what is true. These are serious diseases in an American society which prides itself on its openness and which depends on a viable democracy and on sufficient unity of purpose to cope effectively with complex challenges. These afflictions are endemic, even potentially fatal, a danger manifested in the quasi-fascist persona of a spectacularly dishonest American President and by the sycophantic collaboration of his party.

DEMONIZING THE OTHER

The imagination opens pathways to an empathetic understanding of others: who they are; what they are; and why. Judgment of others should ordinarily be withheld until a serious attempt is made to understand them. This is the best defense against two pernicious violations of the project's morality: dismissing the unique humanity of others by stereotyping and/or demonizing them. The struggles against racism and antisemitism are struggles against these moral failures. Racism and antisemitism are standard examples of cultural phenomena deeply rooted in the world, and, to a most discouraging degree, in the psychological reflexes of many people.

SUPPRESSING CURIOSITY

Curiosity is a powerful generator of self-development, a primary catalyst in the search for truth and understanding. But it can also feed degenerate and evil behavior. Beyond these concerns, a healthy curiosity should be nurtured, especially in young children, and should not be suppressed at any stage in their development. But intentionally or not, this suppression has been happening in those American classrooms in which teaching for the test has virtually excluded imaginative, creative, curiosity driven thinking, a contradictory failure in a society which ostensibly prides itself on fostering creative individualism.

This suppression is not only a problem of misguided policies. Compliant teachers and administrators share part of the blame. But the fault lines spread out into homes and communities. Much blame belongs to an anti-tax driven neoliberal ideology which minimizes support where it is most needed and emphasizes basic skills and vocational preparedness at the expense of the critically important tasks of educating for citizenship and for historical and cultural understanding.

NEGLECTING CREATIVITY

Curiosity and creativity go together. Both need to be nurtured in the young. Both are important in virtually every aspect of their education. Curiosity-driven, creative young people are a valuable resource in every field, and are of particular value to themselves, to discovering themselves, to their own development. But in many schools not only is curiosity suppressed, but creativity is neglected. For instance, when budgets are cut the arts are often the first thing to go, and the arts are an invaluable, though by no means the only way, to give young people an experience in creativity.

CRUSHING INDIVIDUALITY

Powerful forces are always at work pressuring human beings to conform to spirit imprisoning patterns of thought and behavior. This is a nearly universal tendency among ideologies and religions, particularly among the most passionately held and the most rigid. But these forces never quite succeed against the creative independence of the human spirit. In spite of its incessant propaganda and authoritarian practices the Soviet Union ultimately failed in its attempts to excise religion and mold its citizens into the image of the Soviet Man, that exemplary communist, that hard-working tractor driver, that Hero of the Soviet Union. Christianity's historical attempts to enforce conformity need not be reviewed here. ISIS tries to force humankind to surrender in absolute conformity to its aggressively cruel interpretations of Islam.

OBSTRUCTING THE COMMON

The obstructions to the realization of the common are complex and pervasive, present everywhere throughout the world. Flaws in human nature stand in the way: self-satisfied ignorance, narrow minded selfishness, and hatred of the other; immoralities too often reinforced by religion, ideology, and propaganda; and backed up by police brutality and poisonous injections of fear.

WASTE AND THE WASTED

Among the cruelest of the immoralities is the neglect of the wasted, of those whose lives are lost to poverty, disease, and the tyrannies of ignorance.

To participate in the modern consumer culture is to share in the creation of huge quantities of material waste much of it hidden away in landfills and other depositories, beneath abandoned industrial sites, and across rarely traveled stretches of the oceans. The safe disposal of radioactive waste seems nearly unsolvable. Discarded digital devices are loaded with lethal chemicals. Material waste cannot be eliminated but it grows more threatening even though impressive efforts are being made to manage it. To fail to deal with it is a moral failure and risks serious consequences.

In respect to the massive resources they consume and the existential risks they represent military institutions and their weaponry pose a conundrum to the minimization of waste. They cannot be eliminated and are required when certain circumstances arise, when efforts to keep the peace have failed, but they pose an ongoing dilemma of how much and for what. Military preparedness carries with it an underlying threat to the human prospect. The militarization of the planet, which at present is a growing problem, and the waste of critical resources which that entails, must be radically minimized in the decades ahead if a civilization is to be secured which is shaped and energized by the shared commonalities of humankind.

These costs are not only wasteful. They could get much worse. They could drown out other essential commitments. Arms races are now underway, not only in the upgrading of nuclear weapons, but in other 20th Century types of weaponry; for example, in the marvelous new aircraft carriers and in the preposterously expensive new fighter jets now coming on line. Beyond all this, a revolution in warfare is looming which will depend on advances in artificial intelligence and technical breakthroughs, and which may not only make aircraft carriers and fighter jets obsolescent but will require a rethinking of strategy, tactics, and training, as well as massive investments in newer kinds of weapons.

ENGAGING FOR
THE FUTURE

Chapter 4

STRATEGIES AND TACTICS

GIVEN THE DANGEROUSLY fragile situation confronting humankind, attempts to shape the future by means of wars and revolutionary violence present counterproductive prospects. Wars and revolutions typically unleash waves of hatred, cruelty, and indiscriminate destruction. Although the strategies and tactics of nonviolence may require at least as much tough-minded courage as violent behavior, nonviolence is infinitely better wherever it has any chance of success. Minimizing violence in bringing about change not only discourages humankind from ripping vulnerable commonalities to shreds but also minimizes the wastage of human lives and of the natural and built environments.

Violence undermines the moral imperative of mind, imagination, and engagement to understand others as fully and empathetically as possible; to recognize that their religions, ideologies, and cultures are the underpinnings of their life-worlds. Beyond this stress on the importance of non-violence the global project offers no formulaic advice on strategy and tactics, no pithy guidance, no little Red Books. Strategies and tactics depend on the opportunities and the circumstances and must be thoughtfully and creatively worked out. Given the complexities and uncertainties involved, strategies and tactics are at bottom experimental until applied and measured by results.

Although it is ultimately revolutionary in intent, the Global Project is inherently directed toward peaceful long-term transformations. It would be extremely unrealistic to believe that these transformations are likely to be rapidly achieved. Patience is necessary, although patience should not become an excuse for failing to engage. Progress may depend on unforeseeable historic opportunities. But to move forward those who support the project must strive to implant the morality of mind, imagination, and engagement in those around them and show how this morality may be applied towards achieving a humane and peaceful global civilization.

When it comes down to issues of what to do and why, of strategy and tactics, and of solutions to problems posed, individuals committed to the global project may have sharply divergent views, may be facing seemingly irreconcilable differences, may argue passionately among themselves, but because they are standing on the same moral ground and are committed to the same goals, they are positioned to begin to work together in the search for common ground, for compromise, for a modus vivendi, for avoiding civic paralysis. They have placed themselves in a more promising position for creating a better future than the positions in which rigid partisans and ideological absolutists have placed themselves.

Those working to promote the project need to develop whatever strategies and tactics appear to be both appropriate and potentially effective depending on the particular challenges they face and the opportunities presented. They should acquaint themselves with the history of non-violence and passive resistance; and they should study the strategies and tactics of exemplars such as Gandhi and Martin Luther King.

They should do everything possible to discourage violence from their opponents and avoid responding with violence themselves except when confronted by threats to life and limb. They should not attempt to exercise their opposition against contemporary authoritarians in public demonstrations when the only possible outcome is a massacre of demonstrators. There are better ways to build opposition which may be much harder to suppress.

In developing strategies and tactics, it is essential to distinguish between adversaries and potential collaborators. The great world religions, in so far as they can free themselves from intolerant exclusiveness, could become essential collaborators within the project. As stated earlier the project does not take sides in arguments over the existence of God, but it recognizes the fundamental place of spiritual experiences in the story of humankind, and it supports the freedom of individuals to come to their own conclusions regarding religion and religious faith. The morality of mind, imagination, and engagement is not dogmatically secular. It is complementary to the traditional moral codes though not necessarily in the details. The traditional codes are reciprocally complementary in so far as they emphasize the cooperation of human beings in peaceful coexistence and in altruistic behavior.

The morality of mind, imagination and engagement implies cultural struggles but not the dogmatic, strident, demonizing cultural wars of the sort to which Americans have become accustomed; but consistent and determined struggles against cultural attitudes and culturally driven behavior which undermine the project's moral values and which block progress towards the realization of its goals.

The principal cultural challenges are a corrupt political culture; an imperialistic economic culture; a popular culture which is often mindless, violent and frenetic; and an educational culture which narrows the channels of personal development into occupational readiness. The world will not become a utopia of virtue. But each of these cultural challenges must be resisted and diminished because they are formidable obstacles to that freedom and holistic personal development opened up through the morality of mind and imagination and because they stand in the way of reaching the project's goals.

Those individuals whose vocational focus is on serving humankind person-to person, face-to- face, may be among those most open to the 21st Century project and its goals. These may be health professionals, social workers, teachers, and first responders. Or they may be others outside of these loose categories who are involved in altruistic causes. In fact, they may be anyone who has successfully transcended narcissism and greed and is prepared to subordinate self-regard to serving others. Those scientists, scholars, journalists, writers, and artists who are implicitly committed to the project's values and goals could provide essential leadership. Leaders in public and private institutions who are committed to the public welfare could be enlisted. Most important of all are those young people who are searching for meaning and direction in their lives and who could discover in the project's goals and values promising pathways to their self-development and a viable future. Those thoughtful seniors who want to leave behind a more hopeful world could be drawn in.

Developing well-conceived, evidence-based, morally and technically sound initiatives is the most promising strategy for achieving progress. The social media offer possibilities for building global networks. With imaginative leadership and clearly focused aims these networks could grow into global movements which could exert the political and economic pressure necessary to bring about constructive change.

Health-care professionals could build a worldwide alliance dedicated to providing humankind with the best health care possible. They could develop strategies and tactics to make this happen. They could build

     SLIDING PAST THE SHADOWS OF CATASTROPHE

from the bottom up and from the top down through the active participation of committed individuals and through organized initiatives. They could seek to create and implement a common agenda with other organizations and institutions which share responsibilities for the well-being of humankind. Teachers could build a similar worldwide alliance which could coalesce with the alliance of health care professionals into a larger movement which could contribute mightily to the realization of the humanitarian goals of the 21st century project.

It is not possible to single out a particular strategy or a compelling menu of tactics for strengthening the morality and realizing the goals of the 21st Century Project. Strategies and tactics depend on circumstances and opportunities. Some of these are local, within the home, the school, the work-place and the community. Some are macro, within the state, the region, the nation, and the world. Some represent formidable combinations of several or most of these. When it comes to strategies and tactics, hard creative thinking and wise engagement is what is called for. Those committed to the global project must discover what to do and how to do it.

Chapter 5

MANAGING THE DRIVERS OF CHANGE

If a peaceful civilized world is to be achieved, then creative responses to the great 21st Century drivers of change are mandatory. Change comes about in many ways and from many directions and with impacts which are often best understood in retrospect. Climate change may be the most inexorable of the 21st Century drivers of change. Population pressures must be high on any list. But at least five others require powerful imaginative responses. It will be necessary to respond to the destructive undersides of global capitalism; to the divisive separatisms of religious and ideological exclusiveness; to the disruptive impacts of the digital revolution; to the evolving, often chaotic, dreadfully dangerous, world of global politics: and to failures in governance which entrust the future to the dangerous reality of drift. It must strive to influence and even reshape these drivers of change in directions compatible with the morality of mind, imagination, and engagement and the project's goals. If it is to succeed, the Global Project itself must become a relentless driver of 21st Century change.

Global Capitalism

Virtually everyone is economically dependent, including the author of this proposal, on the global reach of the incredibly fruitful alliance of market capitalism, science and technology, professional management, and supportive governments. More comprehensively than any other global force this alliance defines our contemporary world. It pushes forward relentlessly and, in spite of ominous setbacks, it proceeds on an assumption of inevitable success. It hardly misses the mark to claim that at this time global capitalism *is* the Global Project of the 21st Century.

Its utopian vision is clear whether fully articulated or not. It will ride the waves of fresh discoveries, innovations, entrepreneurial energies, creative investing, and managerial competencies to a new world in which every human being will have opportunities for a comfortable life. Most of humankind wants to enjoy the rise in living standards which it seems that only this alliance can deliver. This message is also clear. If it fails, all is lost; there are no alternatives. It must be allowed to develop its own scientific, technological, managerial, and market-driven solutions to the most worrisome challenges confronting humankind. Governments must provide the legal and international context necessary for this success. Beyond that, governments must stay out of the way.

Unfortunately, global capitalism with all its promise may be so deeply flawed, and ultimately so intellectually rigid, that it will plunge humankind into catastrophic debacles. Its dogmatic dependence on growth may misallocate and push the consumption of irreplaceable resources beyond what is required for the long-term wellbeing of humankind. Its rationalizations of greed and of immense accumulations of private wealth, accompanied as these sometimes are with contempt for the less privileged, neglect of the poor, and seizures of public space, could ignite revolutionary upheavals which could destroy the human prospect.

It could even so successfully impose its neoliberal ideological rationale on education and on the popular culture that it would become in effect a benign dictator over mind, imagination, and engagement, impeding the maturity and freedom which are so important to the well-being of humankind.

There are serious thinkers who deserve respect, some of whom are latter day Marxists, who clearly articulate the many contradictions and vulnerabilities in the capitalist system, and who it would be unwise to ignore. These thinkers clearly understand too much. But to the extent that they conclude the system is so exploitative and risky that it must be overthrown, they are not only endangering the creative productivity of the system, and the system's valuable though morally ambiguous support of freedom, but they open the door to catastrophic political, economic, and social upheavals which could make it impossible to achieve the project's goals. The pursuit of these goals imposes the grim task of bringing the capitalist system to heel, of controlling its downsides, of eliminating its monopolies on power, and of implementing levels of clearly justifiable regulation which must drag those who resist into compliance.

The Global Project does not predict the political and economic arrangements which may be in place at the end of the 21st Century. The most promising of these arrangements needs to be gradually and peacefully sorted out through the decades ahead. Those committed to the project must work at influencing and reforming the capitalist driver of change in directions supportive of the morality of mind, imagination, and engagement and of its twin goals; and, if in the long run it should prove necessary, it must struggle to replace it with something else. The capitalist system has been saved more than once by creative responses to its catastrophic failures. Surely, this may happen again; and it may happen again more than once; and in unprecedented ways.

   SLIDING PAST THE SHADOWS OF CATASTROPHE

Science and Technology

A project which is committed to the formidable challenge of helping to create civilized life-worlds for all of humankind cannot rely on scientific and technological fixes, no matter how constructive and successful these may be. For example, artificial intelligence and quantum computing may offer as yet unimagined solutions to all sorts of intractable problems. These are highly significant drivers of change, possibly the most transformative of all in this century; but even the most sophisticated algorithms cannot feed, clothe, or offer humankind the nurturing care necessary to the discovery of meaningful lives and the realization of creative potential. The project assumes that human beings at the end of the century will be much the same creatures as they are today and rejects utopian projects, scientific, technological, or otherwise for remodeling humankind.

The digital revolution's offspring, the robotics revolution, may provide good jobs and high incomes to small elites while pushing whole categories of workers into frustrating lives with little or no employment. If this unsettling prospect comes to pass, then the internalized freedom and moral purposes of the project offer attractive sources for maintaining the self-respect of humankind and avoiding a tragic waste of capabilities and dreams.

We are in the midst of a technologically driven revolution in communications which is holistically transformational, which is impacting every aspect of our lives, and which threatens to bring changes to who and what we are in spite of the fundamental assumption of the project that we will remain essentially the same creatures throughout years ahead. But beyond that still distant shadow, and from the project's perspective, the most important implications of this revolution are, on the one hand, its dangerous tendency through the social media to break humankind down into self-sustaining echo-chambers vulnerable to lies, fake news, and foreign trolls; and, on the other, its networking potential for building and expanding the global project.

WORLD RELIGIONS

The world religions tend to thrive on dogmatic certainty and on the often well-meant though not always publicly proclaimed goal of bringing all of humankind into the fold. They are significant and enduring drivers of change. Each of the great world religions is its own global project for the 21st Century and beyond. They are important drivers of change; but, to complicate the picture, they are also important sources of inertia and of resistance to changes which may be required.

The morality of mind, imagination and engagement implies an empathetic appreciation of the existential role of the spiritual in the life-worlds of millions, of Christians, for example, whose lives are grounded in their faith in Jesus Christ, of Muslims whose spirits are nurtured by their prayerful submission to Allah. It encourages all believers to find a place in a morality centered in truth-seeking which is open to others who are traveling different paths. Their widespread participation will be essential if a civilization depending on tolerance and mutual understanding is to be achieved. Nonetheless, this opening up to others will be resisted by dogmatic exclusiveness and by age old hostilities towards those outside the faith. This resistance may be diminished by patience and persuasion, by the pursuit of mutually important objectives, by the togetherness forced by globalization and the digital revolution, and perhaps, most unfortunately, by catastrophic events.

The project obviously stands against the anti-intellectualism which is by no means universally present in the world religions but is much too common and can be destructively retrogressive. This anti-intellectualism is sometimes manifested in an anti-scientific strand which is usually combined with fundamentalisms of the book. Those committed to the project must resist this anti-intellectualism and should encourage those who find life's meaning in their religions to be open to others who are traveling on different religious and secular pathways. The project rejects any particular program of religious or ideological triumphalism, but it is open to working along with and within the religions and the predominant ideologies towards a collaborative peace without forced victories.

GLOBAL POLITICS

The goals of the Global Project imply the need for international institutions and organizations which are strong and effective enough to build and maintain a humane and peaceful global society without necessarily displacing local values important in the life-worlds of many. Given the geopolitical fragmentations, and dispersals of power, and the endemic hostilities infecting the world of today, establishing these international institutions and organizations either by redesigning what already exists or creating new ones appears nearly impossible. But be that as it may, it is still possible to work towards strengthening and improving international governance, patiently and incrementally, guided by the project's overarching goals. The real world is and largely remains a world of nation states which behave to protect their own interests and still depend on the risky geopolitics of balances of power.

In working towards improving the international order it will be helpful to keep in mind that the international landscape is always changing, and that it sometimes changes in surprising, even shocking ways. Prevailing assumptions are turned upside down. Brilliantly conceived books and articles on the international order suddenly become outdated. The Soviet Union collapses, the Cold War ends, and we were told that the triumph of liberal democracy has marked the end of history, and that we will go on living in a peaceful unipolar world dominated by the benign leadership of the United States backed by its predominant economic and military power. But then what happens? 9/11, endless war in the Middle East, the rapid emergence of authoritarian China as a great regional power with an expanding global reach; the Russian trouble maker keeps on making trouble; terrorism proves stubbornly difficult to eradicate; and nationalistic, racist, and fascist currents arise in seemingly stable societies.

The project must anticipate a shape-shifting world, must look and listen for hints of startling change. Ideas matter. To have a feel for what may happen in the future ideas often prove to be more helpful than short-term fixations on interests, personalities, and policies and on close-up interpretations of events. To anticipate geopolitical possibilities, it may be more useful to step back and look for the ideas which are animating the behavior of particular regimes. What is the philosophy, the world view, behind its various moves, where may they be tending? What are the regimes motivating dreams, however fanciful they may seem? Who are the thinkers that its leaders turn to while mapping out the future in their heads? In retrospect, the history of 20th Century cannot be understood without recognizing the anticipatory power of the ideas of Marx and Lenin, or of Hitler's Nazi roadmap in Mein Kampf.

Can we understand Putin's Russia as well as we might by concentrating on Putin's moves towards authoritarianism, his blatant aggressiveness, his growing list of dangerous, disruptive moves, and his other disturbing acts? Or would we understand all this better if we were less mesmerized by Putin himself, took a step back and examined the ideas which Putin's Russians have synthesized into an approach to governance and to geopolitics which has fitted rather well within the historical experience of the Russian people and which goes a long way to explain Putin's persistent popularity up to now.

Given all that the United States has contributed to the global economy, to peace, stability, and world health; given its many world class

    SLIDING PAST THE SHADOWS OF CATASTROPHE

universities, and its outstanding research facilities; given the entrepreneurial energies and creativity of so many Americans; given a population whose origins reach into every corner of the world, the United States could potentially lead the way through the maze of challenges which lie ahead.

But first, America must come to its senses. It must free itself from its internal divisiveness and hatreds. It must free itself from the ideologically driven partisanships which have come to dominate its politics. It must attack problems pragmatically and in the spirit of compromise. Ideologies always distort reality, as necessary as they seem to be for intellectual comfort, and for rallying a crowd, for opening up careers in politics, but typically they are more harmful than not when infused with rigid short-term thinking.

America will have to move beyond its ideological and political rigidities and reject the mutual demonization of opponents. It will have to turn its back on the lies, liars, and the self-serving truth-deniers who are poisoning its culture. It must free itself from a nationalism which has been poisoned with xenophobic appeals and shallow assertions of American greatness; and it must restore the legitimate pride which Americans have in what they have accomplished at home and in what they have contributed to the peace and prosperity of the world. But the United States cannot lead others into the future unless it sets an admirable example, which at present, in spite of all the pieties of the City on the Hill, it is failing miserably to do.

The moral values and the goals of the Global Project could shape this political and cultural transformation. But for that to happen, it must come about from below, from an awakened American people and from the emergence of leaders who can show the way. Hopefully, that is beginning to happen. The results of the 2018 Congressional midterms were a hopeful sign, but there is very long way to go to heal America's sick political culture. In Part II below, I attack the problem of what the United States must do to get its house in order and to offer world leadership consistent with the project's goals.

GOVERNANCE

Authoritarian regimes have sometimes been notably successful in advancing the economic and security interests of their people, and in maintaining peaceful and constructive relationships with their neighbors, and many a failed democracy has had quite the opposite effects. But the Global Project is not ideologically committed to any type of regime. It is pre-ideological in this regard as in all others. Those committed to the project should judge the polity in which they find themselves according to how tolerant and supportive it is of the morality of mind, imagination and engagement and how well it is serving the realization of the common and the minimization of waste. In so far as possible, they should engage in moving their governments in these directions. This may well be the best way to improve the prospects for creating and upholding successful democratic political institutions. But violent attempts to do so are likely to result in unfortunate set-backs.

The project's commitment to democratic political institutions is indirect because it does not anticipate the institutional arrangements which may be in place by the end of the 21st Century; but its commitment to democracy as the self-evident right of every human being to participate in the governance of their life-worlds is absolute. This right is built into the project's morality and goals. Everyone has a right to self-development which is inviolable and to that radically internalized freedom which that can offer. Strengthening the ties which bind humankind together and minimizing the wastage of healthy meaningful lives is to lay the foundations for strong, realistically designed, legally entrenched, globally extended, democratic institutions. But as things stand today humankind is facing what may be a long indeterminant

        SLIDING PAST THE SHADOWS OF CATASTROPHE

stand-off between democratic and authoritarian regimes. It is by no means clear which is destined to predominate.

In the globalized economy, driven by powerful corporate institutions and controlled by oligarchic wealth, those national governments which are dependent on democratic processes and which lack the sharp teeth of authoritarian rule, are gradually being turned into manageable pests, best left to their endless bickering and perennial failures to get much done. Oligarchic power is also pushing democratic electorates to the sidelines to be kept contented with the contemporary equivalents of bread and circuses and with unfettered opportunities to indulge their ignorance and prejudices.

If humankind is to slide past the looming shadows of catastrophe and successfully manage the great drivers of change, it must be supported by a multitude of inquiring minds, honest truth seekers who will investigate, analyze, propose solutions, and engage; who will open pathways towards a secure and peaceful global civilization.

The Global Project is at least as long as the century, and to think that it must be accomplished quickly would not only be absurd but hopelessly discouraging. Its goals must be pursued and obstacles confronted in ever changing circumstances which will vary from one place on the planet to another. Individuals who concentrate on a particular problem may not to be the same as those concentrating on others; they may be far apart in time and place, may live anywhere in the world, and may step forward at any time. The challenges aren't static. Opportunities for overcoming them will open up at different times, in different places, and from different perspectives of mind and imagination.

The morality of mind, imagination, and engagement combined with

the two overarching goals may be dismissed as offering hopelessly simplistic recommendations for coping with the horrendously complex
challenges facing humankind; but this would be to miss the point that
the Place to Start is not about specific policy solutions but offers an approach to every complex challenge without preconceived conclusions.
It is simplistic in its a priori moral orientation but infinitely complex
in its potential applications to challenges about which it seeks the most
complete understanding, the most plausible interpretations, and the
most persuasive conclusions attainable within the limits of human
fallibility.

The project's overarching goals may be simply stated, but they open
the way to an unlimited range of responses aimed at shaping the future in the direction of these goals. The project's best prospects for
generating support depend on its simplicities. If it were comprised of a
thick manual of principles and a lengthy list of goals, the project would
be unworkable and could be dismissed as another ideologically driven
scheme. By starting from the same place and aiming at the same goals,
it opens up unlimited possibilities for development. Truth seeking,
imaginative understanding, the meaning of the common, the wastage
of human beings, the looming shadows of catastrophe, the great drivers
of change, each of these topics demands consideration which may draw
upon mountains of evidence and immense resources of analytical and
creative thinking. The Global Project assumes that these investigations,
each starting from same place and aiming at the same goals could help
move the future towards a better place.

REDIRECTING AN IDENTITY

Chapter 6

Towards Freedom and Engagement

There is no way to know how many people across the world think in ways consistent with the project's morality or whose engagement with pressing issues is consistent with the project's overarching goals. But we know enough to know there are many people who think and act in these ways. This does not mean that these people are consciously aware of thinking and behaving within an explicit framework called the morality of the mind, imagination, and engagement or that their activities are intentionally supportive of the project's long-term goals. Were they to recognize their personal participation in the project's moral framework and consciously direct their activity towards its goals then they would be positioning themselves to join with others in a global effort to create a viable civilized world.

If a personal commitment to the project is to reach beyond supporting the moral values and the goals to the more difficult task of integrating them into the conscious center of a life-world, it faces formidable obstacles. To succeed at that it may be necessary to sort through such personal baggage as bad habits of mind, imprisoning ideologies, reflexive partisanships, unexamined philosophical and religious assumptions, as well as identifiable personal barriers of psychology and character.

Working through these difficulties is likely to be a never completed task, but it is the road to an enriched identity, to that freedom and distancing which is at the vital center of the morality of mind, imagination, and engagement. From this vital center, the individual is free to stand back, and to think and imagine fresh responses to oppressive externalities, to search for answers to whatever questions may emerge from this orientation of consciousness. This orientation implies determination not to be misled by those simplistic, deceitful, and manipulative answers which are always lying in wait within our contemporary society and culture.

It implies a holistic and imaginative approach to other human beings, an effort to try to understand what made them who they are, what may be driving them, their motives and their goals; to try to discern in them the good, the bad, and the evil, and the shades of gray. This implies caring about their humanity, even of those who must be recognized and dealt with as dangerous adversaries.

It implies engagement in the public forum from consciousness enhancing perspectives which include a paradoxical distancing from political partisanship and ideological rigidities, and an opening up of the search for answers based upon the realization that the best course of action is most likely to be found if evidence is respected, if arguments are carefully weighed, if the sources of information are critically examined, and if the demonization of others and their points of view is kept at bay.

Finally, it implies the cultivation of an awareness of those critically important but subtle obstacles to understanding presented by ambiguity, nuance, and paradox, which, when unrecognized, may make it im-possible to understand other human beings, the world of humankind, the possibilities of human life, the hills and valleys of human history. These have become obscured and even lost from sight in our current culture of communications. Although it is true that it is best to say whatever you may have to say as simply and clearly as you can, there are lurking dangers in making this principle into a cultural fetish. It leads to the sound bite ridden dumbing down of the language itself, to an undermining of clear expressions of ambiguity, nuance, and paradox as essential tools for understanding. Burying listeners and readers in jargon or in big words chosen for effect is off putting and obnoxious but in expressing insight into nuance, ambiguity, and paradox a rich vocabulary may be more helpful in getting at the truth than a starved vocabulary from which useful tools have been excised.

The morality of mind, imagination, and engagement is neither monastic nor escapist. It is not a proposal for hiding away from the world or for rejecting every externality that doesn't fit its moral values. Engagement means engagement and recognizes that virtually every human being, whether mentally healthy or not, is engaged in the externalities of their lives. They live within a culture, multiple cultures really, which feed and shape their life-worlds. The Global Project is an invitation to stand back, look about, and apply the morality of mind and imagination to this cultural world in determining what to do. But this is difficult. Hardly anyone is exempt from the attractions and distractions of the cultural externalities with which they are surrounded. In this author's lifetime, it has become ever more difficult to stand back from the enticing, often beautifully and powerfully presented commercial, political, and popular cultures.

These appear to be engulfing the life-worlds of many, immunizing their sensibilities to the distortions and lies employed to manipulate them, and undermining their capacity for mature reflection. Many appear to find their sources for what is truly real in colorful imagery, dramatic spectacles, charismatic celebrities, and virtual reality; are dependent on sound bites and tweets, on demagoguery and propaganda as their primary sources of interpretation. This has the makings for an exciting and absorbing life-world. Next to this the project's invitation to grow oneself, to enrich identity, through the morality of mind, imagination, and engagement may appear too arduous and unprofitable. It offers demanding effort without obvious payoffs: looking for the evidence, searching for answers, facing up to complexities, reaching out through the imagination into the life-worlds of others.

How should those who have committed themselves to the project relate to the powerful individuals and institutions which surround them, which impinge upon their lives, and upon which they may be dependent? Who, for instance, in the world today is not ultimately dependent on global capitalism? Who, for instance, is not dependent on the sanity of those who have the power to unleash a global nuclear catastrophe? How can committed individuals draw others to the moral framework of mind, imagination, and engagement, and persuade, nudge, or compel entrenched power to support the project's goals?

Ideally, wherever in this world these committed individuals may be, they will be free to speak out, to vote in elections which have not been fixed, and to assemble for peaceful purposes. Ideally, they will not be confronted by artificial barriers to communication or the prospect of retaliation for their participation in the social media. Ideally, they will not be targets for persecution or prosecution or for disdainful dismissals of who they are and what they stand for. Ideally, their rights will be protected by the courts.

But throughout much of the world the realities are quite different from these ideals. Many governments and other powerful institutions are prepared to punish even the most reasonable expressions of independent thinking. Armed with pervasive powers of surveillance and determined to crush unwelcome public demonstrations they make it difficult if not impossible to connect with others whose opinions they regard as threatening.

The Global Project isn't an invitation to martyrdom. Those who are confronted with in-surmountable obstacles should proceed to cultivate their internal freedom and learn all they can about who and what are driving the imprisoning externalities. They should reflect, analyze, imagine, and look for vulnerabilities. They should search creatively for strategic and tactical options. Meanwhile, they should watch and wait, living by their commitments to the realization of the common by treating other people as though they really mattered and their commitment to the minimization of waste by behaving in ways consistent with that goal. They should promote the morality of mind and imagination not through unacceptably risky public activities but by exemplifying this morality in their everyday relationships. Meanwhile, they must be patient and prepare themselves to engage publicly when realistic opportunities should arise.

Even in relationships which are adversarial, even in those which at the extreme may lead to violence, it should never be forgotten that life confronts each human being uniquely, that each is limited by their own conscious awareness. The world they are born into and which confronts them is not exactly the same as anyone else's world, not a sibling's, not even an identical twin's. It may be necessary to fight them and the evils which they support, but that they represent within themselves a minute human universe is a commonality which should never be forgotten.

Reasons for rejecting a commitment to the Global Project are formidable. Not only does the project impose a burdensome respect for truth

          SLIDING PAST THE SHADOWS OF CATASTROPHE

and the obligation to imagine one's way into other life-worlds; but, for a person whose own life is progressing in a satisfactory way, a hard look at the toxic mix of worrisome challenges overshadowing the future and at the institutional rigidities and weaknesses which seem to guarantee inadequate responses is quite enough to invite hopelessness. This commonsense response is understandable: "My problems are in the here and now. What should I do but make the best of things? I'll settle for the challenges of daily life and satisfy my mind and imagination by escaping into the infinitely various, exciting, and pleasurable world of popular culture." But, unfortunately, this does nothing to counter a global drift towards catastrophic outcomes.

Chapter 7

—∾—

ADVICE

IF YOU HAVE committed yourself to the global project's morality and goals, you may now be asking yourself how to proceed. Your answers must be your own if they are to direct your activities and strengthen your identity, but the thoughts and advice below may be helpful.

TRUTH AND INTEGRITY

Do not look on truth as something presented to you by your parents, teachers, or by others, for your passive acquiescence. Truth seeking is not truth. It is a moral activity directed to discovering what is true, as difficult, contradictory, and ambiguous as the results may be. In looking for the truth, always try to begin with the evidence, with the factual evidence, and in so far as possible with the proven facts.

We live in a culture which is becoming ever looser with the evidence, ever more indifferent to the facts. Truth begins at home. Be honest with yourself. Most liars can be counted on to be liars to themselves, on feeding their self-images with self-serving lies, lies which often corrupt their relationships with others. Of course, we wouldn't be human if we didn't sometimes kid ourselves, but mature adults recognize this tendency and control it as best they can.

When considering challenging issues widen and deepen your evidentiary field. Cast as wide a net as you can. Assess what you find as objectively as you can. And be open to whatever seems to contradict your assumptions. Be willing to change your mind. Ideological and religious absolutists claim that they are the real truth seekers. They defend their grip on "the truth" by ignoring or closing off evidentiary fields which support the views of others.

A fact is a fact, but the universe of facts is confusing and opaque. Not every honest searcher for the truth agrees on the facts or when they agree on the facts agrees on how they should be interpreted or on their relevance to an argument. As an honest truth seeker all you can do is the best you can. What matters is the honesty of the truth seeking and the hope that this will improve your competence in sorting out what is true. Often, in selecting courses of action, the best you will be able to do is to look for and act upon the most promising probabilities.

A fact is a fact, and an idea is a fact, but it may be a special fact, a fact which could make an important difference in understanding. A severe limitation on anyone who would control the future is the impossibility of knowing which ideas will do the most to shape it. The discovery of fresh ideas is a benefit of truth seeking. Enjoy your freedom to discover your own ideas. Stay open to those of others, and give theirs a hard and honest look.

Keep reading. If you are to distance yourself from the daily whirl, if you are to reach beyond the immediate offerings of radio and television, as vivid and informative as these may be, if you are to step back from the excited opinionating in the social media, then you will want to read not only for background, for ideas, for arguments rooted in the facts, but for the liberating pleasure of exploring the world of humankind through the words of honest seekers: historians and journalists; economists and other social scientists; novelists and poets; artists and architects; science writers; children's writers; academic writers in fields of interest; and all those other thoughtful and imaginative people whom you find have helpful and worthwhile things to say.

Your reading will be severely limited. You may not have time for more than an occasional book, for an article or two, or a story or a poem. But try to find time for serious reading on subjects addressed by other truth seekers. This will help you step back from what is happening in your lifeworld. If, for instance, you are appalled by America's sick political culture, then read biographies of the Presidents of the United States. Think about what made them who they became, what they tried to accomplish, and what they learned from their predecessors. Most were able people. None were perfect. Some were more admirable than others. All had to cope with complicated problems. Some did better than others. Virtually all, up to the present, sought to defend and preserve their country's basic institutions. In reading about them, look for possible hints of what ought to be tried today.

Aside perhaps from extensive, exploratory travel, there is no better source than literature for reaching out into the lifeworld's of others for empathetic understandings. At its best literature portrays the complicated responses of authentic characters to the unique circumstances of their lives. Whatever cultural world they occupy in time and space we perceive in them their humanity. We see in them reflections of our own.

Clarify your thinking. Do this for yourself. It may be helpful to trade ideas and insights with others whom you trust, but a promising way to discover what you really think is by writing, by hard even painful writing, by sitting down at the keyboard and concentrating as you write, by aiming for clarity and precision, by selecting better words, by stepping back to verify your facts, by reconciling any contradictions, by organizing your ideas, by writing and rewriting until you're satisfied that you've come close to putting into words your best thoughts. Then you may discover that your tweets and text messages have surprising limitations, that they have mostly been little stones tossed off the top of your head, rough cut or polished, unimaginative or creative, but not as successful as you would like in capturing what you really think. Now you may discover that you are composing more clearly worded, better argued messages.

Reflect on your uses of the internet and social media. Avoid addictions. Be very careful on whom and what you trust. Be conscious of the ways these seductive tools gather information which might be used against you. Recognize the manipulative strategies: to catch and hold your attention, to play on your emotions, to sell you products, to capture you politically with clever lies. Keep these useful tools at arms-length. Don't live your life inside them. Take the time to actively engage with real problems in the real world.

To defend your integrity against the liars, manipulators, truth-deniers, and conspiracy theorists who are all around you, unprecedented in their cynical variety, trust your own critical insights. Look for the motives behind these immoralities. They are weapons wielded in self-interest, often by those who know that they are lying. In your search for the truth turn to individuals who have an identifiable commitment to truth seeking and to resisting lies and liars.

Your mother may have been one of those or your favorite teacher and they may have been what you needed to start you off on the right path. But in the search for truth credit must be given to those for whom truth-seeking is fundamental to their work, whose work is judged by peers who expect them to adhere to the highest standards of their craft. Look to the scientists, the scholars, journalists, writers, and jurists who uphold these high standards. You should take them seriously.

This doesn't mean they will hand you truth wrapped up neatly in a box. They are always arguing among themselves and bring different dispositions to their work. Some are conservative, some are liberal in how they look at things. Most are decent people; though some are not. But they are professionally committed truth-seekers. Your task is to give the most credit to those who seem most credible to you, to be standing on the most solid ground. Your judgments are up to you. No one else can make these judgments for you.

These truth-seeking professionals comprise elites, irreplaceable reservoirs of expertise which the world cannot do without, but this does not mean that they deserve the derogatory charge of being "elitists" which is intended to imply that they consider themselves superior to other people and can't possibly understand them. This is propagandistic stereotyping. Most of these "elitists" understand that their fate is bound up with others, that they share their humanity with all of humankind. If you happen to be one of these "elitist" experts yourself, you are a generalist in your commitment to the global project, a person who is trying to understand and cope with the world from beyond the reach of any particular expertise. But this doesn't mean that your expertise isn't invaluable to you and to others in building understanding and in contributing to solutions.

RESTRAINT

As a human being you are connected to your life world by rich and varied emotional experiences, among an unlimited range of possibilities by appreciation and love, by distaste and hatred. You have a right to all your feelings, but in critical matters you must struggle to subordinate them to your search for truth and understanding. Impulses towards vengeance and destruction may seem more than justified, may appear to be supported by the facts; but to act on these, to resort to violence, is likely to make things worse, to undermine the moral values and the goals to which you are committed, and to nurture evil.

PRUDENCE

In determining what's to be done prudence councils caution and humility especially when confronted with choosing among multiple courses of action when the evidence is less than conclusive and the arguments cut in different ways. Global warming failed the prudence test. If many years ago, when it emerged as a worrisome but poorly understood trend, it had been prudently assessed, then long-term horrific consequences might have been avoided. It would have been prudent to have publicly recognized global warming as a potential threat and started to consider evasive action. In spite of Al Gore, whose persuasive warnings reached back into 19th Century science, prudent responses have happened much too slowly and are still massively resisted. Unfortunately, we may be living in the century of drift, of much too little much too late. We are confronted with other looming threats not fully understood which call for more prudent groundwork if we are to avoid being blindsided by catastrophic failures. The failure to take up global warming sooner and more seriously was a failure to look ahead and prepare ways around that menacing shadow of catastrophe.

POSITIONING IN TIME

If your life-world seems exclusively anchored in the present, if it seems indifferent to assessments of the past, if it seems to limit your thoughts about the future to projections of the ever-present now, your mind and imagination may be imprisoned in an existential trap. If you are to break out of this trap; if you are to acquire the internal freedom and distancing necessary to commit yourself fully to the project's morality and goals, then you need to make a conscious effort to widen your time horizons, both backwards and forwards, into the past which has made the world in which you find yourself, and, as imaginatively taxing as it may be, into the longer future which can never be precisely known, which is always enshrouded in thick fog, but which nevertheless presents many identifiable existential challenges to the human prospect.

THE JANUS EXERCISE

Those of you who commit yourselves to extending your time horizons into the past and the future may find it helpful to participate in the Janus exercise, a constructive mind game, which invites you to apply the morality of mind, imagination, and engagement to your understanding of the past and to imagining plausible responses to the challenges of the future. This exercise is named for Janus, the powerful Roman god of time and transitions, typically portrayed with two strong faces chiseled in stone, one peering into the past, the other into the future.

The past offers historical perspectives on what happened, on situations and events, on their causes and their outcomes, and on the personalities involved. Imagining involvement in this past as an observer and decision maker opens up counter factual possibilities for applying the morality of mind, imagination and engagement and the goals of the project to these historical events, personalities, and outcomes. It opens speculative possibilities regarding the wisdom and competence of decision makers and actors and on how alternative decisions might have changed the outcomes. Everything is open to wherever your imagination and insights may lead.

There is nothing scientific about this exercise, but to practice it upon a varied universe of historical personalities, events, and surrounding

 SLIDING PAST THE SHADOWS OF CATASTROPHE

contexts can enhance depth of understanding and maturity of judgment for engaging with the present and the future. History will not tell you how things could have been different. That's for you to speculate about as thoughtfully and imaginatively as you can. Although the future can be expected to present similarities to the past, history does not repeat itself. Facile analogies are risky.

Nevertheless, this exercise will not only immerse you in aspects of the past, and help you realize how complex the world that made you really is, but that even small differences in what actually happened might have had large consequences. To see these may help you see that the small differences you can make may have larger consequences. These speculations are enhanced and gain in plausibility the more deeply resources from the past are drawn upon: not only history and historical biography, but philosophy, literature and the arts, and material remains. Depending on the chosen subject of counter-factual speculation, the sciences and social sciences may be indispensable. Of course, with all the demands upon your life you may not have much time for these counter factual speculations. But they can be helpful even in small doses.

Everything happens in the present. We may interpret the sculptured head of Janus as peering far into the past and far into the future, but the faces of Janus are carved into a rock that never moves. Whatever we do happens in the present, whatever influence we intend to have upon that future in which our lives unfold.

The Global Project does not offer utopian or dystopian visions of the future, but it insists that the shape of future must be worked out over time against all that is unknown and unknowable, guided by the project's morality and overarching goals. That doesn't mean that these visions have no place in your thinking about the future, nor in feeding your hopes and fears about how things will turn out. Useful, virtually indispensable, are visions of the future which have been informed by the moral imagination: Orwell's *Nineteen Eighty-Four*, for example, and Margaret Atwood's *The Handmaid's Tale* and her gripping dystopian trilogy, starting with *Oryx and Crake*. Orwell and Atwood express not only their fears for humankind but tenuous hopes expressed in the courage, caring, and personal loyalties of certain characters. Writing a half-century apart, both insist that much must be changed before it is too late.

MORAL ENTANGLEMENT

The mutually supportive features of the morality of the mind, imagination, and engagement often become entangled with their immoral opposites. The moral and the immoral not only collide in shades of gray, but bleed into each other as colors sometimes do: untruths with truths; fake news with facts; uplifting creations of the imagination with creations which are depraved. These ambiguities challenge our understanding and can make it difficult to distinguish the moral from the immoral.

We do not live in a dualistic Manichean universe caught in the middle of a horrendous battle between the co-equal powers of Good and Evil. In our world, good and evil, the moral and the immoral, are forever engaged in a sweaty wrestling match. In Christian mythology Satan is not a separately created God, but a fallen angel, a rebel against the one and only God. The sources of good and evil are related and entangled. It requires the moral imagination to disentangle them.

In your commitment to the project your approach to these entanglements should be to do your best to recognize them, to interpret them within the moral framework of mind, imagination, and engagement, and to consider their relationship, if any, to the project's goals. Earlier in the text I wrote about how useful recognitions of ambiguity, nuance,

          SLIDING PAST THE SHADOWS OF CATASTROPHE

and paradox can be. You will need these to come to terms with these ambiguous entanglements.

Religious Reconciliation

As a religious person, you may be facing the problem of disentangling your mind and imagination from whatever dogmatic exclusiveness may stand in the way of your search for truth and understanding, and if you are, you may also be determined to accomplish this without undermining that faith which is of transcendent importance in your life-world. This may or may not be possible for you, but it may help to ask yourself this question. "Which is the more compelling in my religion, its insistence on exclusiveness or its emphasis on the universalizing principles of love and understanding?" These values have an important place in most religions and are consistent with the values of the Global Project. The recognition of this common ground may make it possible for you to comfortably bring together in your life-world both your religion and the project's morality and goals.

Ideological Reconciliation

The Global Project assesses ideologies from the pre-ideological platform of the morality of mind, imagination, and engagement. It insists that every ideology is too simplistic, too reductive of an infinitely complex world, and typically so riddled with half-truths and inconsistencies that it is absurd to treat it as ultimate truth, as though it were an enduring conclusive answer to all the questions which arise within an ever-changing world. Nevertheless, as human beings our life worlds are shaped and given direction by ideological systems. We derive comfort and purpose from them. As finite, severely limited creatures, they offer appealing interpretations of a world which we can comprehend only in limited samples.

The Global Project doesn't propose the elimination of ideology. That would be absurd; but it does ask the committed to step back from their ideological predilections and assess them from the perspective of the project's pre-ideological platform. As part of this process, they should ask themselves whether they can relate comfortably to the project's goals.

NATIONAL AND THE TRIBAL RECONCILIATIONS

Virtually everyone lives within national and tribal life-worlds which are essential to their identities. These present a culturally rich but dangerous diversity in the world of humankind. The realization of the common and the minimization of waste does not imply a homogenization of these life-worlds in all their richness and diversity into a global singularity. This would not only be impossible but, were it possible, would be an existential and cultural calamity. The human story thrives on its diversity, on diverse identities. But as with other reconciliations, it is necessary to move beyond the narrowing limitations, in this case beyond xenophobic and chauvinistic national and tribal life-worlds to empathetic understandings of the other and to support the creation of global environments which permit nations and tribes to live together in constructive peace.

This has been the meaning of the struggle to build the European Union, which assumes the nationalities of its members, that the French will remain deeply attached to France, the Germans to Germany, the Danes to Denmark, etc., and that if the centrifugal tendencies which are ever arising among these nationalisms can be contained, then Europe's great experiment can be perfected into a collaborative political, economic, and cultural entity which is stable, peaceful, prosperous, and the happy home of all; and which offers a compelling example to a dangerously fragmented world. But for now, sadly, this remarkable achievement is being undermined by reasserting nationalisms.

If you're deeply attached to your nation and your tribe, you should strive to do whatever may be helpful to bring these attachments into line with the global project. This may be a tall order. It may be very difficult for you, but you still need to do what you can to work towards the project's overarching goals because a viable future for all the nations and all the tribes may depend on it. You need to do your best to reconcile your national and tribal identities with an appreciation of your responsibilities to the wider world of humankind.

Entrepreneurial Creativity

To succeed the Global Project will need the entrepreneurial energies and creative imaginations of individuals across the world in every political, social, and economic context which will allow them room to attack seemingly intractable problems with creative energy, intellectual understanding, organizational and leadership skills, and who can draw together the people and resources needed to succeed. These entrepreneurs may emerge from among the highly placed or from within the poorest communities in which it may appear that there is virtually nothing to work with, but in which an inspired individual will find a way.

In the United States with its fixation on economic growth the emphasis on entrepreneurship is largely confined to the creation of new businesses and products. This is understandable. America's impressive economic success is largely attributable to the energy and creativity of its entrepreneurs. But entrepreneurship is not confined to the world of business and technology. Embedded in the fabric of American life are institutions and organizations serving other important needs, which were created in the first place by talented and dedicated entrepreneurs who recognized these needs and devised creative ways to meet them.

In the discussion of Strategy and Tactics, I suggested that teachers and health professionals, those who care for the well-being of individuals one on one, if they organized themselves into global alliances could move the world in the directions of the project's overarching goals. Creating these alliances would be formidable undertakings which would require the emergence of energetic, gifted, entrepreneurial personalities who could provide persuasive leadership, and would require the building of vast global networks from the top down and the bottom up.

WHAT ARE YOU TO DO?

After considering this mentoring advice and reflecting on its applications, what are you to do? As severely limited as you are, that all comes down to you. What are you to do, from your moral starting place, to make things better within your life-world, better in ways consistent with the project's long-term goals? It's up to you to find your answers. What will you discover if you search for needs and opportunities? What will you find if you look around? What could you do to become fully involved and to stretch your capabilities? Is there a social or political movement which appeals to you and into which you could pour your energies? How entrepreneurial are you? What could you organize? What could you get started?

   SLIDING PAST THE SHADOWS OF CATASTROPHE

BUILDING ON THE PAST

Chapter 8

EDUCATION

DRAWING AUDIENCES AWAY from the liars, the cynical manipulators, and the perpetrators of hate, who now dominate many media sources will depend, in part, on expanding the audiences for those radio and television programs, those newspapers, magazines, and books which these dishonest sources like to dismiss as elitist and unreliable, but which, in fact, often admirably represent the morality of mind, imagination and engagement in their commitments to truth-telling and in their concerns for the well-being and future of humankind. But to expand these audiences, nothing could be more helpful than the transformation of education in the direction of the project's moral values and overarching goals.

At its best education struggles against the wastage of human beings, against poverty, against empty lives, against violence to the self and others. Imparting vocational skills necessary for survival is integral to that purpose. But to virtually reduce the purpose of education to training economically productive individuals, as demanding as that task may be, is narrow and shortsighted. It shirks responsibility for providing resources and guidance for holistic self-development, for those qualities of mind and imagination which underpin meaningful lives and constructive citizenship.

Moreover, it seems virtually oblivious to the digital/robotic revolution which may lead to a catastrophic scarcity of jobs even among the highly educated. If this happens, then how should the perennially unemployed be educated? A society enriched by the digital/robotic revolution should be able to protect them from abject poverty. But should education concentrate on preparing them for a life of ease, for their role as consumers, for popular culture's mesmerizing offerings? Or should it prepare them for a mature adulthood, for understanding themselves and the world around them, and for improving the prospects for those close to them and more broadly for humankind? The answer to this final question may not be as obvious as it may seem. The affirmative would support an educational system which would deliver thoughtful individuals prepared to question the status quo. That could seem unacceptably risky to those in power.

Preparing the young for mature adulthood requires curricula rich in the humanities and social sciences, in history and literature, in civics, in economics, and in global understanding; which nurture creativity in the arts and crafts; and which prepare them for the meaningful use of their leisure time and for volunteer activities. Rebalancing curricula in these directions does not imply the neglect of science education. Nothing may be more effective in teaching evidence based truth-seeking to the young than teaching them what science is all about, as a self-correcting truth-seeking enterprise, and of how science's devotion to truth-seeking has shaped and is shaping the world they live in.

THE TEACHERS AND THE SCHOOLS

The transformation of education in the direction of the project's morality and goals will depend on the participation of those responsible, particularly, and most critically, the teachers. Whatever the subject being taught, the best teachers teach by example, by their excitement, by their curiosity, by fresh perspectives in searches for what is true, by their insistent referrals to the evidence, by their questioning, by their listening, encouraging, and responding to their students, pleased with their creativity, and sympathetic as they struggle with ideas. By teaching in this way, the teacher exemplifies those understandings and empathies which contribute to a broadened life-world and to constructive citizenship. Moreover, the teacher is pointing toward the realization of the common and raises barriers against the wasteful emptiness which threatens their students' lives. The teacher encourages freedom in her students of the most fundamental kind, the freedom to shape their own life-worlds, a freedom resistant to ideological indoctrination and cultural shallowness, a freedom to discover what is meaningful for them.

Experienced teachers know that their teaching will not necessarily catch hold; but if they exemplify these values, greater numbers of thoughtful young people will go out into the world who are curious, who respect hard evidence, who demand honesty and transparency from their leaders and institutions, who are caring, and are much harder to manipulate with propaganda and appeals to prejudice.

Nationally and globally the education enterprise is so huge, so complex, and involves so many people, in its broadest sense a substantial proportion of a population, that to generalize, though not entirely futile, is intellectually risky. But if the project is to achieve a constructive global impact on education innumerable strategic and tactical challenges must be addressed. Ultimately, these strategies and tactics will depend upon the teachers, and must be implemented in the contexts in which they do their work: "contexts", a word loaded with a vast array of structural, organizational, social, political, economic, and cultural implications.

All sorts of people become teachers, most work hard, most care about the subjects they teach, and most are committed to their students, to their learning and general well-being. The education of teachers, their classroom training, their skills, their personal characteristics, their capacity for relating positively and constructively with their students vary enormously.

For any approach to have much chance of moving the astonishingly diverse global educational enterprise in the direction of the moral values and goals of the project, it will have to be persistent, patient, strategically and tactically astute, and, above all, catalytic. If this change is to happen at all, it will be largely brought about by teachers who are at least implicitly committed to the project's values and goals, teacher leaders who draw their colleagues in, and who are looking for opportunities to infuse these values and goals into the educational enterprise. This catalytic effort will be strengthened if the teachers take a fresh look at who and what they are. To do this, it may be helpful to keep certain thoughts in mind, to reflect upon the following admonitions which may not readily occur to those attempting this fresh look. (Note #4)

Try to think of the educational institutions in which you work, at whatever level you may be teaching, as standing in an upside-down relationship to you. Think of the structures of authority in which you work, not as looming above you, locating you at the bottom of a hierarchy, which has been modeled on the needs of government and business, but as belonging conceptually underneath you in the supporting role because these structures have meaning and consequence only in light of the work you do. This is a self-imposed trick of the mind and imagination because, of course, you will not be able to completely free yourself from the hierarchy in which you work. In truth, accountability alone demands a reasonable measure of subordination.

To succeed at the constructive transformation of education which you are working towards, you need to adopt this upside-down outlook and hold on to it with great insistence. You are not an expendable laborer, a retail associate, or a minor bureaucratic functionary, at the bottom of some private or public hierarchy. Your place is quite different from that and rests on your having a large say on what is taught and how, a fair measure of intellectual freedom, and a stable and supportive environment in which to teach which reaches out beyond the school itself. All this you must insist on.

You are morally obligated to teach the subject you have been hired to teach and to treat the curriculum you have agreed to teach with appropriate respect. But whatever else you do trust your own mind and imagination, your own experience, your own powers of reflection, analysis, and synthesis, the implications of your own reading and research, your own dreams for yourself, for those close to you, for your students above all, and for the wider world. If you don't do that, if you don't insist on your right to do that, you have surrendered your claim to the status of an independent professional and you may not get very far in your efforts to make things better.

THE UNIVERSITIES

No other institutions are more important to the success of the Global Project than universities, both domestically and globally. No other institutions in American society are as strongly positioned to insist that truth-seeking rooted in the evidence is, in fact, a moral and social imperative, and that knowledge so derived must not to be lied away. The universities need to make every effort to implant these values into a sick political culture and to undercut the pernicious influence of lies, liars, and anti-intellectual truth deniers. This needs to be an overriding goal unless the universities are prepared to settle for a future as self-protective fortresses permanently at risk. Truth-seeking and the

     SLIDING PAST THE SHADOWS OF CATASTROPHE

dissemination of knowledge stand together as the core mission of every university worthy of the name, no matter how extensively a university may be caught up in a multitude of other responsibilities. Under the burden of these, this core mission, though real, may seem to languish in the background, but it must be forcefully and publicly articulated if the university is to be fully mobilized in its own defense.

The universities in the United States have been centering their attention as a predominant priority on welcoming and protecting highly diverse populations, and on integrating them into their communities--a critically invaluable service to the students and to society. They have been steadily improving their services and redesigning their curricula to meet the wishes and needs of students. But in light of the existential challenges which confront them, the universities must concentrate attention, inside and outside their walls, on protecting, explaining, and advancing their core mission. It is now possible, for instance, for many undergraduates to explore a menu of introductory courses and then to take advanced courses in a major without acquiring more than a foggy notion of where this learning comes from or what it has taken to discover and develop it. By teaching about the requirements and costs of truth-seeking and, when possible, by making assignments to reinforce this teaching, more students could be drawn to truth-seeking as a personal standard. It could strengthen their resistance to lies, liars, and other anti-intellectual crusaders. It could encourage them to defend the core mission of their universities.

Most American universities are applying their core missions, their teaching and their research, to creating a safer, socially and materially more viable world. To focus some of these efforts, they could do no better than to pursue the goals of the 21st Century Project which are consistent with what is best in their internal cultures: first, the minimization of waste, the wastage of human beings and of the life supporting conditions upon which humankind depends; and, second, fresh understandings of the common, of shared commonalities and of how these may come to be embedded in social and cultural values, and in political and economic arrangements. No other institutions are as strongly positioned by mission and by culture to provide global leadership in the pursuit of these essential goals.

LIFELONG LEARNING

The Global Project is an existential invitation to engage in lifelong learning through the morality of the mind and imagination and through searching for the realization of the common and the minimization of waste. This learning can be nurtured by reading, listening, observing, and reflecting; by thoughtful communications through the social media; by conversations with friends, neighbors, and at work; by participating in churches, clubs, volunteer organizations, political parties; and, perhaps most helpfully, in the formal education venues, the schools and the universities. Whatever approaches to lifelong learning may be chosen, these need to be directed towards developing that internal freedom and distancing which is at the center of the project and to strengthening resistance to ideological rigidities and lies, while remaining tolerant and understanding of others who are taking in the world from different perspectives.

To strengthen lifelong learning in the direction of the project it may be necessary to create fresh institutional arrangements to provide support. These could offer classes and workshops through which participants would engage in the challenges and difficulties of applying the morality of mind, imagination, and engagement to complex issues.

Besides these formal learning opportunities, personal mentoring could be at least as valuable in extending and strengthening participation in the project. Many individuals who have accepted the project's existential invitation to pursue their self-development through the morality of

    SLIDING PAST THE SHADOWS OF CATASTROPHE

mind, imagination, and engagement, could use personal help in this demanding process. This could be provided by other sympathetic individuals who have worked their way through to an understanding of the challenges and difficulties, discovering for themselves effective ways of dealing with them. Mentoring could be conducted one on one or within small groups. It could lead to the emergence of quasi-professional counselors who would help individuals deal with their challenges in depth. This could cross the lines between tutoring and psychotherapy, and, were this to happen, would have to be squared with the standards and procedures of the psychotherapists.

Chapter 9

AT THE CENTER: THE HUMANITIES

THE 21ST CENTURY Project offers a cutting edge which reaches into and across all the fields of study, including the sciences, the social sciences, the humanities and the arts. It advocates the moral framework which underlies them all and overarching goals which must be pursued if the existential challenges of the 21st Century are to be successfully managed and overcome.

The reader may need to be reminded that "the humanities" is a general term for several fields of intellectual and cultural creativity, each of which seeks understanding within its traditions and its evolving methodologies, each of which develops its own modes of expression, and each of which continues to evolve in new and sometimes exciting directions. The humanities include history, literature, philosophy, and the arts. The sciences teach us what we are as biological creatures and explain the evolutionary processes which have created us. The social sciences study our behavior, its causes, and its connections to reality; and draws socially relevant conclusions from its findings.

Among the humanities and the social sciences, all of which offer valuable insights into understanding what we are and what has made us who we are, the two most essential, for a grounding in the Global Project may be history and literature. History, the antidote for amnesia about the past, enriches the context for decision making in the present and encourages prudent considerations of potential consequences. Literature opens windows to imaginative participations in the life-worlds and experiences of others, people like your neighbors or like strangers in strange lands, human or humanoid, attractive or odious, familiar or weird, beckoning to you for your admiration or disgust, for your love or your terror.

As it inexorably rolls on, history is full of warnings and advice. It is forever challenging every ideological attempt to impose a particular structure on reality, advising it to be aware of changes in the landscape, obvious or subtle, which may be undermining it, which may be turning it into something different from is origins, which may overthrow it in the end. Soviet communism, which claimed to offer the final word in historical understanding, became dead in the water and finally succumbed to overpowering changes in the real world. Could the United States be headed in a similar direction? Vicious politics? Political paralysis? Declining institutional legitimacy? Science denial? Short term thinking? Let's hope not, but the red lights are flashing. We had better take the messages of history seriously.

For many centuries, science was included in the book of knowledge as that branch of philosophy called natural philosophy. But as science and technology made incredible advances, this subordination of science to philosophy grew hopelessly quaint. In the 1950's the British scientist and fiction writer C. P. Snow argued in an influential lecture that an irrevocable split had occurred between The Two Cultures, between the culture of the humanities and the arts, and the culture of science and technology. This widely accepted, though always controversial argument, may have helped to free science from the nonsense and ideological obstacles embedded on the other side, but the Global Project implies that it is time to turn full circle, that the time has come to recognize that both these cultures, as different as they most certainly are, should not be segregated into separate worlds of mind and imagination.

Each field of study approaches its subject matter through its traditions and its methodologies. Each is motivated by internal debates. Each is sometimes critical and dismissive of other fields, but all are driven by curiosity, all depend on a quest for what is true, and all move ahead through creativity and imaginative visions of possibilities; and, finally, all depend on the intellectual and imaginative powers of the human mind. All fall within the purview of the morality of mind, imagination, and engagement. And, because they all represent the work of humans they all depend on the viability of the societies which support them.

The Global Project is mildly imperialistic in its understanding of the place belonging to the humanities in the universe of knowledge. It argues that this place is roughly analogous to the place given to theology in medieval Europe as the Queen of the Sciences. This assertion is not intended to give the humanities the hierarchical superiority over other sources of knowledge which was once given to theology; that would make no sense at all; but it is to suggest that all these sources of knowledge, including the hard and natural sciences belong within the humanities as an appropriate principle of inclusion. They should all be included together because they are all products of the minds and imaginations of human beings, of truth-seeking, curiosity, and creativity. They all have as their primary goals the advancement of knowledge and understanding, and in their ethical legitimacy they all depend on their service to humankind.

No doubt there will be considerable resistance to the contention that the humanities, as marginalized as they have become, should be promoted into this principle of inclusion. The claim will be made that the humanities are a precious side show in the universe of knowledge. They may be interesting, pleasurable, and pleasantly decorative but are taken truly seriously only by sophisticated elites, found mostly in academia, individuals who may communicate brilliantly among themselves; but whose outpourings are of little relevance to the hard, revolutionary dynamism of the 21st Century, to its science and technology, its globalizing capitalism, and its popular cultures.

The case can also be made against the humanities and the liberal arts (in which the humanities have a central role) that history proves that they have failed to humanize, and because they have failed to humanize have earned their marginalization. It will be asserted that western civilization has been shaped by Christianity and by the humanistic traditions of the classical world, but this has not prevented catastrophic cruelties. Those European elites who supported the imperialistic exploitations of other peoples were formally educated in the classics; but neither their religious upbringing nor their mastery of Latin and Greek stood in the way of their inhumane treatment of other human beings whom they considered inferior to themselves; nor did it keep them from leading Europe into the disastrous wars of the 20th Century. For these failures, as well as many others, the humanities have been pushed into the margins.

The struggle to humanize has always been incredibly difficult and undermined by failures. The barbarians are always at the gates. To compound the problem, the humanities seldom contribute clear cut instrumental answers to much of anything. They tend to defy the formulaic. But in making decisions affecting the future of humankind, when mature, well informed, judgement is required for choosing what is better among instrumental options, the humanities, along with the social sciences and other relevant fields of study, nourish the context in which these choices are made. They may not offer answers to what is to be done, but they offer insights, possibilities, and warnings into the process in which the judgements of what to do are formed.

As the principle of inclusion, the humanities belong back at the center of truth-seeking and understanding, as an essential humanizing proposition. In this proposal, the humanities as the principle of inclusion is virtually synonymous with the morality of mind, imagination, and engagement.

Chapter 10

GLOBAL PROSPECTS

THE GLOBAL PROJECT for the 21ˢᵗ Century is composed of a cluster of inter-related moral values which are intended to guide individuals in their self-development by enriching and expanding their understanding and by encouraging them to engage in improving the prospects for humankind. This engagement needs to move in two interrelated directions: first in the promotion and defense of the morality itself; second, in the realization of the project's overarching goals

The project depends on consistency, firmness of purpose, and on patient hard work through a time span that may be expected to include several generations of participants continuously adjusting strategies and tactics to emerging opportunities. Whatever the contingencies, these participants will need to remain confident that the most promising pathways to a peaceful and humane global civilization are through the project's morality and goals.

The project is neither utopian nor dystopian; it does not offer a comprehensive vision of the world at the end of the 21ˢᵗ Century. The prospects for achieving a humane and peaceful global civilization do not appear promising. Fundamental questions must be answered. Will humankind remain attached to tribalism, nationalism, and cultural exclusiveness? Will it allow itself to be led by ideological and religious absolutists; by sowers of hatred; by corrupt self-seeking politicians; by those who believe that marketing is the solution to everything; by those who will do or say anything for face-time in the media; or by these in weird mixtures? Will humankind remain ambivalently mesmerized by violence, and continue, however enviously, to condone the triumph of greed? Or will humankind successfully distance itself from these self-destructive traps? Will it gravitate towards nurturing curiosity, truth seeking, and mutual understanding; towards fostering freedom, generosity, and the power of love? Most critically, will it respond wisely and in time to slide past the menacing shadows of catastrophe?

The project rests upon the hope that human beings in sufficient numbers will freely choose to cultivate their personhood through the morality of mind and imagination; and engage in the common destiny of humankind in ways which reach beyond themselves, beyond their own time and place and situation, and will act with the necessary courage. This is the hope; not a hopeless hope; but the margin is razor thin!

The project's success should not be expected to mean that today's world would be replaced by a virtually unrecognizable world. The project leaves imaginary worlds to utopian and dystopian visionaries. The story of humankind has never been composed on a blank slate. For those who take the trouble to look, the past is always discernible. It is visible in who and what human beings have become and in their surroundings. The past lives on in the present, however obscure the connections, however hidden the causal chains. If the project is to succeed it must be in a world which is in many respects a recognizable reflection of today's, though considerably more civilized and nurturing.

     SLIDING PAST THE SHADOWS OF CATASTROPHE

No matter how successful the project might be in helping to build a humane and peaceful global civilization, its success will not be final or complete, a utopian moment frozen in time. It will still be encumbered with partial successes, pockets of failure, and infinite loose ends. That's the way it is with human beings, their institutions, and all their other social and cultural constructs. As long as the human story goes on it will keep changing. The project will be successful if it has helped to instigate and shape the process of building a humane and peaceful global civilization; if it has helped to nurture this movement into a self-sustaining state which continues to support a viable life-world for humankind into the 22nd Century and beyond.

The project points the way to reconciliations of the most dangerous and deeply rooted sources of conflict bedeviling the planet. It argues that universally shared experiences of the human spirit transcend religious and ideological particularities. But it also recognizes the universal human need to live within intellectual, spiritual, and cultural homes. The project does not deny this need. It encourages all of humankind to open the windows of their intellectual, spiritual, and cultural life-worlds and look beyond into the wider world, to perceive others in holistic ways, to empathize with their humanity, and to commit themselves to placing toleration and mutual understanding on solid foundations.

This proposal for a Global Project contends that the morality of mind, imagination, and engagement, and its long-range goals offer an approach to the future which is virtually mandatory if daunting obstacles are to be overcome and the world is to become a better safer place by the end of the 21st Century. This does not suggest, however, that it will necessarily matter if this particular proposal dies stillborn in the cloud. The approach offered would be hopelessly naive were it not for all those civilized human beings who in outlook and behavior conform in many ways to the morality and the goals articulated in this proposal. Should their numbers increase and should they come together to sharpen their mutual understanding, to minimize waste, and to work towards the realization of the common then a "better place" may be achieved.

The project, even if it were to gather considerable support, would not necessarily make an appreciable difference in 21st Century outcomes. Failure: utter failure, dystopian failure is entirely possible. To foresee this possibility, it is only necessary to turn to that usefully dramatic cliché, the worst-case scenarios: the triumph of demagogic politics; an overheated planet; genocidal uprisings and perpetual war; food and water catastrophes; pandemic diseases; an irremediable financial collapse; the disappearance of digital connectivity; geopolitical fragmentation and breakdown; educational decay and a worldwide collapse of educational infrastructure.

If humankind survives a catastrophic 21st Century only to find itself enveloped in a new Dark Age then the morality of mind and imagination will need to be revived if a humane and stable global civilization is to be at last achieved. Hopefully, these values would not be completely lost, but would be revived in ways both old and new. To turn to a well-known analogy: learning was preserved in the monasteries in the West after the collapse of the Roman Empire. The monks preserved important texts. Universities emerged and added to intellectual capital by drawing upon the remarkable culture that unfolded in the early centuries of Islam. A spiritually, imaginatively, and intellectually rich medieval civilization became the foundation for the centuries-long emergence of the modern world.

     SLIDING PAST THE SHADOWS OF CATASTROPHE

CONCLUSION PART I

Now, as always, we are on the edge of an uncertain future which, as always, will blind-side us with happenings we could not foresee. But we would not be human if we did not try to squint through this thick fog of uncertainty for hopeful outcomes, however tempted we may be by dystopian despair. After far too many years in which avoidance and drift have had the upper hand, the pressures are growing to face up to the existential threats of the 21st Century. What is to be done before it is too late will require all the wisdom, patience, and determination that humankind can marshal, if, as an endangered species, we are to reach the end of this century in a better safer place.

PART II
AS AMERICANS WHAT MUST WE DO?

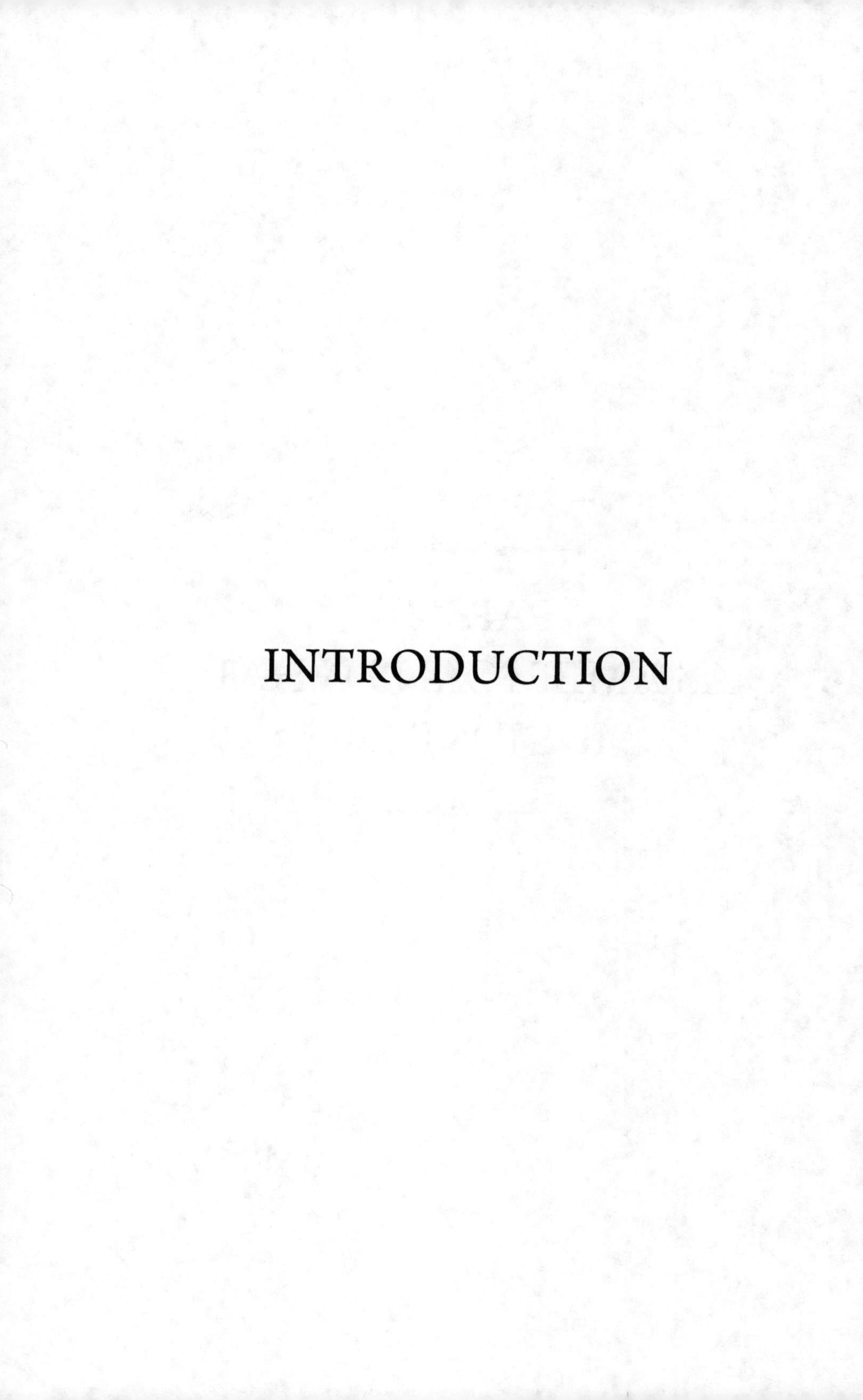

INTRODUCTION

In Part II, I present my thoughts as a patriotic American on what must be done to successfully face up to the most serious challenges which my country faces. Others, living elsewhere on the planet, living in their own distinctive life-worlds must, in their own way, apply the morality and values of the Global Project to the challenges confronting them and the societies in which they live. It is this consistency of approach which could draw humankind more closely together over time.

Earlier in the proposal I argued that America must come to its senses, for its own good, and if it is to become a persuasive example for others. My ideas for bringing this about are derived from experiences which are not exactly the same as anyone else's: the people I have known, the books I have read, my absorption since a teenager in history and current events, and the directions I took in my career: teaching American government and world history in a public high school; serving as a writing coach in a residential college which focused on public policy; teaching the humanities to undergraduates; and a Ph.D. dissertation on the coming of the First World War, that nasty global surprise, that catastrophic breakdown of the international order, which gave shape to the remainder of the 20th Century, to many further horrors as well as remarkable achievements.

Of considerable influence on my thinking have been the twenty-five years I spent as the Executive Director of the Michigan Humanities Council which gave me an opportunity to become well acquainted with my state, with its diverse population, its universities, colleges, and schools, its governing institutions, its museums, libraries, and historical societies. It also meant regular trips to Washington for meetings and events sponsored by the National Endowment for the Humanities (NEH), and many days on Capitol Hill visiting with members of the Michigan Congressional Delegation and their staffs, reporting the Council's work and advocating for the missions of NEH and the State Humanities Councils. These experiences showed me that there were many decent people in the Congress although it also showed me that many of these were too self-limited and constrained by ideology, partisanship, and personal ambition.

State Humanities Councils are non-profit organizations controlled by boards of directors. They receive support from the NEH which, broadly speaking, oversees their work, as well as from state governments, business, other non-profits, and individual contributors. Along with much else, my work with the Michigan Council proved to me that conservative and liberal board members can set their partisan leanings aside to collaborate cheerfully and collegially in serving a common mission. That conclusion was reinforced by my experience of serving on, and for a time as president of Friends of the Capitol, a citizens committee which included partisan professionals from both sides who collaborated in a catalytic role to bring about the restoration of Michigan's fine old 19th Century Capitol building and then in helping to protect the impressive results. Today's common mission is to restore and protect the global lifeworld of humankind, a collaborative undertaking without precedent. In the service of this mission, rigid nationalisms, tribalism, and ideologically driven partisanships must necessarily be set aside.

My proposal for what the United States must do is not tied to the prevailing partisanships, nor formulated as a menu of policy proposals. It is mostly confined to particular angles of attack on America's sick political culture. It is my attempt to dig into what seems absolutely basic if my country is to get its house in order; if it is to have much chance of sliding past the looming shadows of catastrophe.

We Americans are troubled by what is happening to our country. Many are afraid. Even those who lives are going well understand that much is wrong. Many are self-limited by short term considerations. Many are easily misled by lies, liars, conspiracy theorists, fake news, and demagoguery. Many support policy panaceas poorly connected to the facts, pitched at them by partisan ideologues, lobbyists, and self-aggrandizing media gurus enriched by special interests. No wonder so many Americans are prepared to strike out in directions which may be self-defeating, not only for themselves, but for their children and grandchildren whose futures depend on long-term national and global problem solving if the many worrisome challenges of the 21st Century are to be faced up to and successfully addressed.

The potentially catastrophic challenges are well-known to everyone who pays attention to the facts, to all who concern themselves with the accumulating evidence: the growing impacts of climate change, the re-emerging danger of nuclear war, of cyber war as a 21st Century weapon of mass disruption, of terrorism as an easily achieved dramatic act; of the ominous possibilities of pandemics, of shortfalls of food supplies and fresh water, of massive crisis driven migrations, of rising xenophobic nationalisms, of genocides, of all these risks and more within a geopolitical environment which is changing, and may change in surprising ways, but which calls for effective responses which are global and long term.

What must we Americans do to face up to these global challenges? What are the imperatives for the United States if we are to successfully find our way through the decades ahead? Today the United States is still the richest and most powerful nation on earth and is still in many ways the most influential. But wealth, power, and influence are not solutions. They do not show the way past the looming shadows of catastrophe to a better place. That calls for leadership, for global leadership which can earn global trust and help devise evidence-based collaborative solutions to the most dangerous and disruptive challenges.

As individual Americans the place to start is with ourselves, with the morality and goals of the global project. This opens pathways to enhancing our identity as Americans, as exemplars of what is best in our civic culture, of our commitment to make our democracy and constitutional system work, of our right to develop and express ourselves, of our obligation to listen to each other and to reach out towards what we have in common, and to do our best not to leave anyone behind. These, in turn, carry with them an obligation to defend our American identity against those who would undermine it with lies, propaganda, and hatred, who would paralyze and distort it with ideological and partisan purities. This is how we may encourage others who are living under quite different value systems to gravitate towards our values, values which we have recovered our capacity to exemplify.

MAJOR OBSTACLES

Today the United States is trapped by domestic partisan warfare, by an overreliance on military and economic preponderance, and, perhaps most inhibiting of all, by focusing its attention on short term considerations. If the United States is to provide global leadership which paves the way to better outcomes it must seriously look beyond tomorrow towards the days and years ahead if it is to manage its way through and around the shadows of catastrophe, if it is to concentrate its immense capabilities on helping to create a global future which will serve its own well-being and that of others.

Short term thinking aided and abetted by polarized special interest politics has put the United States in a much less promising position to solve its problems than if it had faced up to discernible problematic trends years ago and behaved prudently, cautiously, and experimentally to take evasive actions, to have begun to cope with these problems in spite of uncertainty as to how critically serious they might become. Now, to use an ancient cliché, the United States struggles to close barn doors after the horses have stampeded out. The worst might have been mitigated, if years ago, pragmatic, bipartisan steps had been taken to begin to address the emerging threats of climate change; the cluster of legal and moral issues surrounding immigration; the murderous dimensions of the gun culture; the failures of education within a cyclical pattern of panaceas; and other transformational challenges discussed below. Unfortunately, this neglect has meant that the United States has drifted into serious troubles, raising the likelihood that what may be done will be much too little much too late. Returning the wild horses to the barn will not be easy

Too little too late is virtually guaranteed if America's paralytic partisan standoff isn't broken. There is no magic solution to this sad state of affairs, but it may be helpful to look at it as a disease of the political process, long untreated, which has finally trapped the political system in an iron lung, to use a grim analogy from the pre-vaccine treatments of polio. It is still breathing but it is dreadfully incapacitated. In Part II it is my intent not to promise a cure, but to suggest what might be tried to treat this disease.

Americans tend to lean in one of two directions in their political orientations, to the right or the left, towards conservative or liberal values. Many, perhaps most, lean ambiguously and inconsistently in both directions. They do so because powerful values overlap. Virtually everyone believes in freedom (as they understand it), in democracy (as they understand it), and in the constitutional order (as they understand it), and share pride (selectively) in much if not all of the country's history. Generally, those who lean more or less consistently to the right are Republicans, to the left are Democrats.

Both these leanings have been essential to a healthy democratic process driven by competitive ideas and popular appeals but pushed by necessity towards dialogue and compromise, a political system which has been able to cope with serious every-day problems and face up to the larger challenges of depression, war, and social and cultural change. Decisive action has typically required accommodations between these leanings and has tended to push aside extreme positions. Unfortunately, this healthy road to decision making has been disappearing. Big controversial decisions are being made by a majority party marching in lock step. Though legal, this undermines the popular acceptability of a decision and means that there is a good chance that it will not stay in place, but will be back on the table when the excluded party wins a majority. This threatens a self-defeating cyclical process, a churning of issues which gets the country nowhere, and can't be in anyone's interest except those profiting politically and economically from the paralysis.

Racism is a real, divisive, and radioactive obstacle to curing America's deeply divided political culture. Considering all the wise and thoughtful people who are struggling with this problem, considering the seemingly futile efforts to move beyond it, all that can be done, and must be done, as far as I can see, is to bring all the empathetic understanding to this issue as we possibly can and to realize that what must be dealt with are not only the remaining fallouts from institutionalized slavery, but the anxieties and hatreds of those who have become racist in their white exclusiveness. The most promising responses may be indirect, to help those burdened with racism, real or imagined, to find confidence in their futures and in an inclusive life-world. For this to happen political reform and imaginative public policies may be required.

The United States must set a truly compelling example to the world. Self-satisfying illusions of America as the City on the Hill; complacent beliefs in the United States as the one Indispensable Nation, will not cut it in the boiling cauldron of these times. They will not, if the United States is perceived as a gradually failing democracy, corrupt and half paralyzed; as long as trust in America's reliability is waning across the world. If the United States is to discover its proper leadership role in the 21ˢᵗ Century; if it is to offer a truly compelling example to the world, it must first face up to its own internal problems, to the transformational changes which are necessary both internally and in its international posture.

American Imperatives

These are the overriding American imperatives. The United States must achieve constructive reforms in each of these domains: the political, the economic, the geopolitical, the educational, the social, and the moral. The "moral" raises an off-putting flag. After all, most Americans try to uphold moral values in their daily lives; but, nevertheless, the morality of mind, imagination, and engagement must be included because it underlies responses to each of the other imperatives. Each can be separately considered, but they overlap, interrelate, and, collectively, are necessary targets for attention. The world owes the United States a huge debt. But as important as this is to a proper appreciation of the past, the United States has yet to define its place in the world history of the 21ˢᵗ Century. This process of redefinition needs to be worked out in accord with the project's morality and goals.

Chapter 11

RECOVERING OUR POLITICS

As things now stand in late 2019, the best hope of moving the American political culture in healthier directions will be to rebuild the moderate middle in both major parties with individuals who represent the normal liberal and conservative leanings, but who refuse to be fixated on partisan ideologies and on the self-righteousness and demonizing which now have the upper hand, and will work side by side, honestly, rationally, and in a spirit of compromise to tackle the real present and long range problems confronting the country and the world. This in itself, as things now stand, would be a benign revolution, and could move the country in the direction of a better future. There is much working against this; but hopefully it will be tried.

That failing, then the next best move will be to launch a political movement, virtually a new political party unlike any seen before, an organization which would promote an agenda unlike the typical party platform, those cobbled together lists of vote-seeking policies. This movement would concentrate its efforts on institutional reforms. It would struggle to re-legitimize those institutions of American governance which have been progressively de-legitimized in the eyes of many Americans and much of the world by a large assortment of liars, truth distorters, self-serving manipulators, partisan ideologues, media propagandists, and oligarchic purchasers of power. Over the long run, nothing will be more important to a healthy American democracy, to the well-being of the American people, and to the world leadership prospects of the United States, than the perceived legitimacy of America's principal institutions, not only governmental, but others as well.

The Party of Reform would, of course, be deeply concerned with issues of public policy but in its relationship to these issues it would not expect its members to adhere to a party line. That could confuse its reformist priorities. It would leave them free to define their own positions on these issues. But it would expect them to do two things. To help identify and define structural challenges and to assess proposed solutions. It would encourage them to interject these two angles of consideration into the political process and into public discourse. Reform would be the predominant purpose; relationships to public policy would be flexible, evidence based, and pragmatic.

The Party of Reform would necessarily have to be patient and persistent in the slow hard process of building up support. Winners of elections, however few and far between, however outnumbered, would serve as gadflies for reform, articulating its necessity and struggling to build support.

Comprehensive structural reform may require constitutional amendments, but not of the unwise and potentially damaging kind which have been repetitively proposed as political talking points: term limits which would sacrifice the invaluable experience of senior members of Congress; balanced budget amendments which would reduce the financial flexibility which Congress must have, if it is to respond quickly and effectively to changing circumstances. Nor would it require a constitutional convention. That potentially disastrous option must be avoided. The goal must be to improve the constitutional system of governance, carefully and cautiously, to bring it up to date so that 21st Century challenges can be wisely dealt with. A constitutional convention would be a risky role of the dice. It could throw open the door to a messy ideologically driven rewrite which could destroy the sturdy document we still depend on.

The leaders of this party of reform, would need to determine in consultation with the public, what, if anything substantial, could be accomplished through the legislative process or through the courts. But once these possibilities appeared exhausted, they would need to turn to constitutional reform. For whatever they proposed, legislatively or constitutionally, they would need to come up with exactly the right language, never forgetting that each word can affect the future. Poorly drafted law can cause more problems than it solves. The Founding Fathers drafted a masterpiece, not perfect, but written in clear precise language which has withstood the test of time.

Without popular support the reform proposals would end up as a bundle of futile gestures. Winning popular support would be a long hard fight requiring leadership from the top down and, most critically, from the bottom up, from the enthusiastic input and support of millions. It would require patience, persistence, and imaginative approaches to achieving the critical mass support necessary to bring about comprehensive structural reform. I can imagine the reformers at every level turning to the Preamble to the U. S. Constitution as an inspirational starting place in their advocacy of structural reforms. I can imagine them encouraging their audiences to reflect on the Preamble, on its words, on its parts, and on its meaning as a whole.

THE PREAMBLE

We the People of the United States, in order to form a more perfect union, establish justice, ensure domestic tranquility, provide for the common defense, promote general welfare, and secure the blessings of liberty to ourselves and our posterity, do ordain and establish this Constitution for the United States of America

I can also imagine them proposing additional language to the Preamble which would explicitly set forth the People's expectations of their government, of the standards of behavior necessary for the realization of the "more perfect union".

THE ADDITIONAL LANGUAGE

To make certain that these broad purposes are pursued with transparency, integrity, and courage, and to guarantee that this our Constitution remains the living expression of our will, adapted in the spirit of the Founders to the evolving challenges of history and time, We the People of the United States, establish these expectations for our Government, for the Executive, Legislative, and Judicial branches, that we be told the truth, the whole truth and nothing but the truth, so that our Democracy can flourish in an environment of sound debate; that our Bill of Rights be respected so that our freedoms are secure; that our public officials from the highest to the lowest serve with diligence, competence, and honesty, encouraging by all their words and all their actions the reasoned patriotism and civic engagement of ourselves, the American People. (Note #2)

By expressing an ideal intent this imagined addition to the Preamble sets the stage for attacking the substantive challenges of comprehensive structural reform.

The reformers would need to identify and study the serious structural weaknesses and political/cultural conditions which seem critical to them. For attacking these they would need to find the right language and develop effective strategies and tactics. They would need to develop comprehensive plans. What follows is my own open-ended list of potential targets. The reformers might focus on some or all of these and/or on others not suggested.

POTENTIAL TARGETS FOR REFORM

…The Money Problem. Money has become an all-pervasive poison, corrupting democracy in multiple directions, and allowing disproportionate power to oligarchical self-interest. If money in politics is to be considered an expression of free speech, then policy antidotes to its destructive power must be found legislatively or constitutionally.

…Protecting the Right to Vote. Voter suppression and the manipulation of election results must be stopped if faith in the democratic process is to be fully restored. No other reform is more important than this.

…Truth in Politics. Putting the best face on their actions and opinions is the normal and acceptable behavior not only of politicians but of most people most of the time. It is an essential feature of the art of politics even though it often involves distortions of the truth. Thoughtful citizens must judge as best they can how persuasive these presentations actually are and how closely they reflect what they understand to be the truth. But this normal political behavior is being overshadowed by the demagogic showmanship of Donald Trump. Truth no longer matters. Evidence no longer matters. The law hardly matters. Lying is a tactical weapon. Twitter a system of delivery. And big endlessly repeated lies are a strategy for the inspiration of the gullible.

A democratic political culture depends on a respect for fact and law however debatable the facts, however controversial the law. The weakening of this respect is a cultural disease. The advocates of structural reform had better not ignore it. It demands a creative search for remedies. Records are being kept of the ever-growing totals of Trump's lies and of his cavalier attitudes towards those laws he considers inconvenient. But he appears to be insulated from the consequences of these perversions as long as his avid supporters don't care. Ways need to be found to better protect the place of honesty and truth in our democratic politics. We must not allow the Trumpian mentality to provide the template for our future leaders.

…Leveling the Playing Field. A flourishing American democracy requires a more level playing field which reduces the sense of alienation felt by so many Americans. This will require reforms in education, social programs, taxation, and much else, reforms which will need to proceed, at least implicitly, in the direction of the global project's goals of realizing the meaning of the common and minimizing the wastage of those who experience themselves as left behind. Structural reform in the political culture should open the door to other necessary reforms.

…The Electoral College. The electoral college requirement has meant defeat in recent cycles for two presidential candidates who won majorities of the popular vote. It has meant the concentration of campaign resources in "battleground" states while other states have been neglected or even written off. Eliminating the electoral college or perhaps replacing it with something else could guarantee election of a president by a national majority. It could move the nominating process to a national primary. It could challenge the presidential campaigns to develop national, rather than state selective or, say, city versus rural strategies. Presidential candidates could be compelled to pay attention to the larger interests of the country. But at cross purposes to all this is the bedrock constitutional principle of federalism: each state, however large or small its population, is a unique polity of equal importance to every other state.

...The Congressional Districts. It is a prerogative of the states to define their Congressional districts. This has meant that much of the country has been gerrymandered into safe districts. Incumbents remain in office as long as they toe the party line and are under little or no pressure to prove to their constituents that they are well enough informed and thoughtful enough to debate issues of public policy with an opposing candidate who has a fair chance of defeating them. This may be changing. There is movement in the country and the courts to correct it.

...Overcoming Stalemates. The reformers would need to pay serious attention to those unresolvable cultural issues which poison the political culture, which draw attention away from existential threats, and contribute to governmental paralysis and drift. Right to Life and Right to Choose are driven by passionately held moral positions which the law cannot resolve. One can imagine that if Roe/Wade is overthrown, the legal struggles within and among the states will only get more bitter and more unresolvable than now, keeping the courts busy for another generation. If no compromise-based settlement is possible, then both sides owe it to the future to reach some sort of modus vivendi to set the conflict aside and let the country move on and focus on challenges which are more pertinent to survival.

Much the same may be said in regard to the tensions between the right to gun ownership and the requirements of public safety. This is also a cultural as well as a political and legal issue but given the rising mayhem it appears to be more amenable to mutually satisfactory solutions than the conflict between Right to Life and Right to Choose.

...The Dysfunctional Congress. The Congress has broken down into partisanships that are often so ideologically rigid and bitterly opposed

     SLIDING PAST THE SHADOWS OF CATASTROPHE

that it is extremely difficult to reach important policy decisions based firmly on the evidence and explained clearly enough to the public to win enduring support. The Republicans have been more responsible than the Democrats for this political paralysis, for the emergence of a winner take all ideological mindset; but this denial of equal responsibility doesn't cure the diseases of the political culture. That will require a complex transformation away from excessive partisanship to those patriotic commitments succinctly laid out in the Preamble to the United States Constitution.

It will also require the erection of effective defenses against the overly assertive role of powerful special interests in the work of Congress. They should not be given veto empowered roles in the drafting of legislation. They should not be allowed to turn members into virtual dependents by providing those campaign contributions which must be raised or permitted to enforce this dependency with intimidating threats, usually left hovering in the background. The beneficiary of their largess knows if she displeases her backers, she may face an opponent in her primary more amenable to them. As things now stand, the burdens of dependence can absorb paralyzing chunks of time and energy which ought to be devoted to legislation and useful oversight.

Congress unintentionally ceded to the special interests an oppressive power to interfere in its work when it passed sunshine laws intended to accommodate the indisputable right of the American people to know what their representatives are doing and where they stand on important issues. But the trouble with these laws is that they went too far in imposing transparency onto the sausage making legislative process which often requires meetings behind closed doors in which members are free to proceed collegially, insulated from their partisan publics, to consider all sorts of amendments, and to float whatever good and bad ideas which come to mind. Instead, this well-meant transparency has a divisive and paralyzing effect on the process. It has meant that a powerful special interest like the NRA could sit in on these meetings and record anything and everything it doesn't like, however trivial, and then use against a member.

Lobbying in itself is an expression of the right, even the obligation of Americans, to let their government know what they like and don't like, what they want done and why. It is an invaluable long-standing feature of democratic governance. But it has exploded as a professional activity, especially in Washington, where it depends for much of its legislative leverage on legalized political bribery. It has tightened its grip on Congress by presenting immensely lucrative career destinations for helpful members. This has become a large patch of quicksand in the swamp. Nevertheless, ordinary citizens should be encouraged to appeal to their government either on their own or in organized ways. The messages they send are essential to good governance.

Too many members of Congress are placeholders who appear responsive to the following admonitions: Load up on special interest dollars, no matter how much obsequious cooperation this may take. Be responsive to your voters. Listen to their problems. Always seem as supportive as you can. But don't try to broaden their understanding of the issues. Exploit their ignorance and their prejudices in the name of representing them.

Don't bother with the legislative fine points. Make sure that your funder's pet proposals are included in the bill. No need to read it all. Simply support your party's position tacitly or, when called upon, with passionate sincerity.

Don't miss those televised hearings devoted to political messaging. Make use of your face time. Diminish with angry questions that public servant across from you. Shake your head contemptuously at her answers.

    SLIDING PAST THE SHADOWS OF CATASTROPHE

By pursuing your responsibilities in these ways, you will please your base, prove what a great job you're doing, raise ample funds, and get yourself re-elected. As you know, there are many other members of Congress who take their responsibilities seriously. But let those fools make unpopular decisions, work themselves to the bone, and pay the price.

... Competence as an issue. Congress was designed for simpler more slow-moving times. Is it capable today of serving the long-term interests of the American people? Or is the complex, rapidly changing world of the 21st Century running away from this basic democratic institution? Are paralysis and incompetence two sides of the same coin? These questions must be explored by the reformers. This at least can be said. Broadly speaking, the members of Congress have more formal education than in the past. But do these members represent the mix of credentials needed to wisely confront the challenges of these times?

Of course, Congress can call on every imaginable type of expert for advice. But is it collectively well equipped to digest and make the best use of this advice? It is understandable that as a legislative body Congress is predominantly composed of lawyers. In their committee assignments these lawyer politicians often accumulate considerable understanding of the subject matter. They can be very effective. But does Congress contain enough well qualified people from other fields to make it likely that genuine expertise and deeply relevant experience will be given a front row seat in dealing legislatively with the emerging complexities of the 21st Century?

Many Americans who are eminently qualified in science and technology, in corporate and public management, in the higher reaches of academia, and in other demanding fields and are not necessarily politically ambitious and who are likely to be reluctant to expose themselves and their families to the unpleasant hassle of contemporary politics, but who, if they were candidates for office, could improve the quality of governance. A Congress which included more of these established experts and fewer lawyers could improve its capacity to deal with the intricate technical complexities of the contemporary world. Outstanding political leaders might be discovered among the more reluctant volunteers. The Party of Reform could recruit and support them. Those elected could become Congressional gadflies for reform and could be expected to propose evidence-based policies aimed at the common good. Those out of the sciences, for example, could advocate more well-placed funding for basic science research at a time when others are beginning to outstrip us to our likely disadvantage.

…The Campaign Culture. Campaigns for office typically depend on raising money from self-interested sources in exchange for implicit obligations. That's old news. That's a big problem which must be attacked. But attention should also be given to the typical campaign's dependence on professional handlers, pollsters, advertising specialists, numbers crunchers of all sorts, and a wide assortment of hangers on and political hacks, all doing little or nothing to enhance the public's grasp of the important issues and its chance of wisely judging the competence and authenticity of the candidate. People ask themselves: who is this person running for office; what can I believe she will actually do? If only she didn't seem so engineered and so advertised; if only I could see her through the campaign fog, the partisan-driven hype, and past the manipulative machinery?

… Running against Washington. Presidential candidates, and others, have found it profitable to claim to be running against Washington as virtuous outsiders who, when elected, will drain the putrid swamp. This is a pernicious deception. As soon as they decided to run for office, these candidates voluntarily entangled themselves in the political web. They became aspiring insiders the instant they announced their candidacies, when, to use an old but apt expression, the moment they

          SLIDING PAST THE SHADOWS OF CATASTROPHE

tossed their hats into the ring. Mostly they get away with this deception, a pose which can be seasoned with flamboyant promises. But typically, once elected, little changes. The candidates discover that it is necessary to act within the existing system just like all the other politicians. If the political world is a swamp, then they must find their place among its denizens. The pernicious result of this silly dance is that by basing their campaigns on these specious promises candidates are debasing the government's legitimacy and sowing public cynicism.

...Starving the Argument. Even the most serious candidates, who refer audiences to detailed policy proposals on their websites, tend to campaign in simplistic generalities, carefully targeted, and endlessly repeated. Not only is this what they do, it is what they feel compelled to do. But these condescending simplicities can come across as disconnected from the gut infesting challenges so many people face. They can come across as self-serving calculations, not as genuine responses to these troubles. Unfortunately, this opens the door, as we have seen, for a demagogic personality to bypass the hard issues of public policy or to tear them away from their factual base, and to substitute tough, decisive, entertaining promises to make everything great again for those who see in him a lifeline to hope and self-importance.

All this suggests that the way candidates are connected to the voting public needs to be thought seriously about. Two interdependent possibilities might be considered: first, to more tightly focus political campaigns on discussions of overriding issues, on ventilating them in greater depth; second, to support these discussions by requiring reasonable allocations of time from the licensed media. Each discussion could be focused on a critical question of local, statewide, or national significance.

These discussions could augment and possibly replace the present system of presidential debates. Each discussion would require a situational understanding of an overriding issue. If properly moderated they would not allow the candidates to filibuster their way through with sound bites, lies, and irrelevant asides or to indulge in ad hominin attacks on their rivals. A candidate would be expected to show a broad and detailed understanding of the issue, to have ideas for dealing with it, and be prepared to talk about it in the give and take.

Obvious challenges like climate change or health care might be addressed, but other less obvious topics could reveal even more about a candidate's leadership potential. For example, questions on governance could be asked. What are the federal government's responsibilities for addressing economic inequality? What are its responsibilities, and what are its tools, for protecting privacy? For protecting the right and the opportunity to vote? What about power? Who has it and how is it being exercised in American society? Are there imbalances? If so, what is the role of the Federal government in addressing these? What is the role of the United States in the world today? What are the priorities? Which approach to international relations should be emphasized, the bilateral or the multilateral, and why? What can the United States do, if anything, to encourage authoritarian societies to protect human rights and to become more democratic?

Demands like these would be resisted at every level, by politicians, who would have to do their homework and would be forced to think comprehensively and on their feet, by the media, which would be required to allot time which could cut across their partisanships and hurt their ratings, and from popular prejudices against policy wonks and boring discussions. Nevertheless, these attempts to impose thinking in depth could move the political culture in less mindless, less ideologically driven directions, and contribute to the election of better prepared candidates.

... The Presidency. Reform requires a cautious look at what the Presidency of the United States has become as it has changed through

     SLIDING PAST THE SHADOWS OF CATASTROPHE

historical circumstances and under the shaping impacts of its occupants. The challenge is to guarantee that the Presidency remains firmly rooted in the constitutional structure of American democracy and law and that its occupants behave wisely and courageously in the interests of that incredibly diverse entity, the American people. And in doing so, that they check their prejudices, their narrow ideological predilections, and even their egos at the White House door.

… The Supreme Court. The Supreme Court is the ultimate guardian of the Constitution, of individual rights, and of the democratic process. It selects cases for review which present important legal issues which need to be resolved. It makes decisions which honor its precedents. To guarantee its traditional grip on soft obedience, these decisions must be seen to reasonably apply in a world which the Founding Fathers could not have envisioned.

A healthy viable court includes justices who lean philosophically in conservative or liberal directions and whose decisions are fought out along these lines. But the court cannot afford the impression that decisions are depending less on wisely constructed interpretations of the law and more on ideologically driven partisanship. This impression has been a growing for some time and has been reinforced by the Senate's dodgy refusal to take a vote on Judge Garland and by the two Trump appointees, technically qualified, but selected from an ideologically driven list.

Traditionally, the makeup of the court has been determined by Presidents selecting competent nominees acceptable to their parties, who after thorough vetting's have usually been approved by members of both parties, a bipartisan result which has contributed to the perceived legitimacy of the Court. If the Court becomes too ideologically skewed, too rigidly partisan, then pressures will grow to expand its membership, to make it more amenable for dealing wisely and constructively with critical contemporary issues. FDR ran into a fire-storm of criticism when he tried to "pack" the court to protect the New Deal, but the reaction now could be more muted if the court comes to be viewed as insensitive to social realities and/or obstructionist in dangerous circumstances.

...Equal Justice for All. Judges should be free to judge according to the circumstances, to determine the length of sentences without un-reasonable restraints. Mandatory sentences are often arbitrarily cruel. Every effort should be made to close the enormous gaps in sentencing influenced by such irrelevant factors as race, class, and wealth. The dif-ference in the slap-on-the wrist treatment of white-collar crimes which have sometimes injured millions and the lengthy jail time for less inju-rious crimes such as drug possession is a national disgrace.

...The Administrative State. Electoral and congressional reform could lead to a thorough but fair assessment of the functioning of the Federal bureau-cracy, an investigative study which would be careful not to demonize the dedicated over-burdened people who, for the most part, are making the various elephantine systems work, who deserve more respect and compen-sation than they receive. It would aim to make these systems more efficient and responsive. It would aim to reduce the irritating reasons why so many Americans hate their government for what seems to them mountainous piles of rules and regulations, applied in knit-picking ways, and incom-prehensible without lawyers and accountants. Of course, these percep-tions have been baked into the American people by anti-big government propaganda; and can be countered with the truism that governance in an increasingly complex world requires increasingly complex responses. But if the American people are to have more trust in their Federal Government then this problem of alienation must be addressed.

Public information campaigns would help. The American people would be more supportive if they had a better fact-based understanding of what the federal agencies do and why, and how their performance should be assessed. But this would not be enough. As things now stand, Congress passes laws which are often poorly drafted, overloaded and out of focus, then leaves it up to the agencies to prepare whatever rules the agency finds appropriate for the administration of the law—a reasonable but flawed arrangement. The more elaborate the rules, the more responsibility the agency takes on for monitoring their application. Complexity is in the interest of the agency. It helps build its case for additional personnel and funding.

Congress needs to take this process in hand by limiting new laws to whatever language is necessary to clearly lay out its purposes; by providing explicit guidance to the rule makers to keep them from piling on non-essentials, by carrying out its oversight responsibilities by monitoring the results, and by being prepared to require sensible adjustments. This could lead to less burdensome rule making.

Congress also needs to try to reduce public alienation by permitting bureaucratic personnel to exercise good judgement when applying rules, and by allowing exceptions for irrational or unjust applications. We know all too clearly the injustices that can occur when the exercise of good judgement is taken away from public servants. By taking judgement away from judges by requiring mandatory sentences for petty drug offenses we loaded our prisons and ruined the lives of thousands of young people who did not need to be incarcerated. Now we are witnessing the cruel obscenities of a government which splits up families by deporting the parents of young children.

Public officials could be granted circumscribed room to make exceptions to avoid unfair and unnecessarily cruel applications of the law. They could be required, for instance, to cover these presumably rare decisions with explanatory memos for the files. The morality of mind, imagination, and engagement cannot be taken away from anyone. We should not want to take it away from public servants. Fairness is an abstract value; but the government will not win back the respect of alienated Americans without supporting it. Of course, there would be mistakes, abuses of the greater latitude, identifiable inconsistencies; but it could make things better; and in the bureaucracies it could enhance professional self-respect.

…Civic Education. Much of the American public appears to have little detailed knowledge of how the American constitutional system is designed to work or of how it has been successfully preserved for the last two hundred years by amendment, by congressional and presidential leadership, and by judicial interpretation. This ignorance sets the American people up to be misled and victimized. This ignorance weakens the foundations of our institutions. American government can be taught in a fair, balanced, fact-oriented way, a constructive way which avoids any attempt at indoctrination in a political ideology (aside from a belief in the validity of the American system) or any stress on partisan opinions. I know that this can be done because I've done it, as has my wife. I taught American Government in a public high school in a conservative suburban community, and no one ever attacked me for how I went about it. My wife had a similar experience. She taught American Government and practical law in a public high school in our rural Michigan community. Teaching with an emphasis on substance will be more successful in teaching citizenship than those shallow civics courses which make patriotism their overriding purpose but neglect the knowledge base.

If the reformers addressed these and/or other challenges in effective ways, then the American people could come to understand that what takes place inside their nation's capital isn't happening in a distant world from which they are cut off. They could come to see that they are intimately involved in whatever happens there, that hardly anything could be more American than what goes on inside that beltway which

    SLIDING PAST THE SHADOWS OF CATASTROPHE

encircles the agitated critical mass of America in action. Everything collides there: hopes and fears; knowledge and ignorance; brilliance and stupidity; the honorable and the corrupt; altruism and selfishness; generosity and greed; great wealth and grinding poverty; good and evil in many forms. They could come to see that it is out of this agitated critical mass that their future is being shaped, for better or worse, sometimes with explosive energy.

They could come to realize that a part of themselves lives within the beltway: among the thousands of interest groups, within the offices of those who represent them; and, most critically in their personal interests, in their hopes and fears, their future prospects, and those of their loved ones. They may not care to think about it, but as long as they are Americans, what goes on inside the beltway is integral to their own life-worlds; and calls for their thoughtful, critical, and future directed involvement. (Note #3)

If the structural, political, and cultural reforms initiated by the Party of Reform took hold, then a new normal could be expected to emerge, which, it may be imagined, would mean a reversion to the two-party system which, in the United States, makes more sense than any other. Whether these two parties would be called Republican and Democratic wouldn't really matter because those who leaned conservative and those who leaned liberal would tend to line up on opposing sides. But the new normal would be new because the parties would be operating within a transformed political culture.

Chapter 12

RECOVERING OUR LEADERSHIP

THE BEST CHANCE of shaping a peaceful inhabitable world by the end of this century lies in commitment to those overarching goals, the realization of the global common and the minimization of waste, particularly of the environment on which human life depends, and of the lives of those who may otherwise end up among the wasted; and finally, on the reduction of chauvinistic, xenophobic nationalisms and a decision, however controversial, to look squarely at the doctrine of national sovereignty, which, as fundamental as it is to the nations themselves and to the world order, may be too rigid and inflexible to permit the necessary transformations into a viable and humane global society.

If the United States is to successfully exercise global leadership throughout the remaining decades of the 21st Century, then it will need to concentrate attention and resources on getting its own house in order. Otherwise, the probabilities keep increasing that whatever it does will be much too little much too late. And it must deal wisely with the perennial tensions in American foreign policy between an idealistic impulse to export America's commitments to freedom, protected rights, and democratic polity, and a realistic determination to take the world as it is, to be primarily concerned with existential issues arising, in part, from imbalances in global power. Recent attempts to export democracy with military force have been disastrous and have resulted in seemingly endless wars. But, on the other hand, America's "idealism" was invaluable in nurturing the "free world" coalitions which contained the Soviet Union until the end of the Cold War.

Attending to balance of power issues, backed up by military and economic strength, remains necessary in the world as it is today, but if humankind is to come to a safer better place by the end of the 21st Century this approach to geopolitics is severely limited. Paradoxically, it's too status quo, too unimaginative. It doesn't adequately connect to the looming shadows of catastrophe. Moreover, balance of power competitions could bring about that ultimate catastrophe: nuclear annihilation. Less dramatically, these competitions encourage expansions of conventional armaments, which are not only wasteful, but when driven by fear, may spark suicidal wars.

The United States must take the risk of positioning itself out in front of others. It cannot afford to surrender to a self-destructive culture of retreat. This will require patience, persistence, and courage. It will require backing global institutions which are strong enough and supportive enough of the common interests to help pull humankind together and to struggle against whatever threatens to tear everything apart. It will require foresight and planning to avoid catastrophic setbacks and it will require a commitment to help manage the great drivers of change which are giving shape to the world's future.

Although this proposal will strike some readers as hopelessly idealistic and naive, it is not motivated by utopian visions but by practical considerations. It does not assume a beneficent transformation of humanity; but assumes that human nature is destined to remain a volatile mix of good and evil in an imperfect world. It is a proposal which reaches out towards a wisely governed world, towards the creation of whatever institutions, properly checked and balanced, may be necessary to bring this world about; but it is not a proposal for world government in which sovereign power would be so concentrated that it would overrule the national and cultural life-worlds of most of humankind, thereby laying the ground-work for global tyranny.

The issue of sovereignty, of its sane distribution and humane applications, is critical. The global leadership of the United States rests on the assumption that the United States will maintain its strong position as a sovereign nation; but to lead the way to global stability and peace it must be more prepared than it is now to grant specific measures of its sovereignty, limited and clearly defined, to international structures. If the United States should fail in its efforts to lead, then it must be prepared to yield to others with better methods and ideas.

In his brilliantly persuasive book, *A World in Disarray: American Foreign Policy and the Crisis of the Old Order*, Richard Hass takes on the principle of sovereignty, arguing that it must reach beyond the narrow chauvinistic nationalisms now on the rise, and be reconceived as the principle of sovereign obligation, as a self-imposed requirement on the nation state to take into account the impact of its actions on others and, more generally on the future of humankind. If the nations were to adopt and scrupulously adhere to this principle of sovereign obligation many global problems could be effectively managed. Perhaps that would be enough to assure the global future. And the United States could take the lead by explicitly committing itself to the principle of sovereign obligation and by laying it on the table in all its international relationships. Richard Hass's proposal, as deserving of adoption as it most certainly is, may not go far enough. The principle of sovereign obligation may not generate sufficient leverage to avoid destruction and bring into existence a viable and stable global order. This may require

     SLIDING PAST THE SHADOWS OF CATASTROPHE

the transfers of sovereignty to international entities which are strong enough and widely supported enough to manage global responses to disruptive challenges.

The sovereign nations of the world have made substantial loans of sovereignty to international entities charged with explicitly spelled out responsibilities in the treaties establishing them. The international order depends on these. Mostly, these entities are firmly in place. Many have been around for decades and are rarely controversial. But, at least theoretically, these quasi-sovereign loans are easy to ignore and can be taken back by dissatisfied signatories. The international institutions of the 21ˢᵗ Century which must face up to worrisome global challenges and, if called upon, with managing crises in the relationships among sovereign states, may need to be placed on more solid foundations than those provided by the present network of treaties.

The United Nations, for instance, may need to be reconstituted, or replaced with a more securely empowered entity. To consider this possibility at all is likely to raise the horrifying specter of a tyrannical world government. But that is hardly a danger in a world in which most of humankind is deeply attached to their nations and their tribes, attachments which are likely to remain intrenched throughout the rest of this century. Tyrannies imposed within nations and within tribes and by nations and by tribes are the greater threat, as is the emerging possibility that giant capitalist entities will impose their will, dangerously, but hopefully more or less benignly, on every aspect of late 21ˢᵗ Century life.

What must the United States do? What must we do to help lead the way to a more humane and peaceful international order? What must we do to get out in front of others? What must we do to lead by example? What are the implications of these aspirations for that delicate but all-important issue of sovereignty? How might the principle of sovereign obligation be made more mandatory on the nations than it is now, made more difficult to ignore? How might certain international entities be granted sufficient authority to fulfill their necessary roles in facing up to the 21st Century?

To lead by example the United States must get its political, economic, and cultural house in order. It can't afford to drift along in a quasi-paralyzed state, guided by backward looking policies, while China, in particular, is moving rapidly ahead in responding to 21st Century challenges, in infrastructure development, in alternative energy, in electric cars, in basic scientific research, and in technological education. At least in these responses, China is looking more like the future, while the United States is looking more and more like the past. Given America's huge potential, given all that it is contributing even now, given the humane values for which it has usually stood, it doesn't have to be this way. But if the United States is to look like the future, if it is to lead, if it is to step out in front of others, it must wake up, break loose from short term thinking and act dynamically with creative foresight.

How would the United States do this? What could it do beyond constructive engagement with opportunities, situations, and events? It could seek to leverage the future by creating appealing alternatives to the status quo. Speculative possibilities can be imagined which ought to be kept in mind even if they are unrealistic at this time.

The United States could adopt a constitutional amendment which would permit the delegation of delimited grants of sovereignty to international institutions, grants which would be more difficult to withdraw than those loans of sovereignty granted within the present system of treaties. It might require, for instance, that a sovereign grant could be withdrawn only after the decision was approved by two successive Congresses. Withdrawal would remain possible, national sovereignty would demand it, but it would require lengthy consideration, and could not be done by a President acting alone. This would strengthen the position of the selected international institutions. Other nations would be encouraged to take a similar approach. This would at least encourage others to commit themselves to the principle of sovereign obligation.

Needless to say, a proposal this radical has virtually no chance of serious attention any time soon. But in this regard, the reader should be reminded that this essay is about facing up to the 21st Century throughout the decades ahead, and that events, especially catastrophic events, may force the realization in the United States and elsewhere that reallocations of sovereignty, something like those proposed, must be granted to international entities for the sake of global survival.

The United States could take calculated risks. It could, for example, confront the ever-present danger of a nuclear Armageddon by taking the lead in reducing the massive stockpiles of nuclear weapons which now represent exponential overkill. It could do this by systematically reducing its own stockpiles according to a clearly stated transparent long-term plan, a plan which could be accelerated, slowed down, frozen, or even reversed depending on the responses of others. Integral to the plan would be reductions and redeployments of delivery systems. It would at no time leave the United States in the position where it could not respond in kind to a nuclear attack. Mutually Assured Destruction (MAD) would not disappear. But this American initiative to reduce stockpiles and delivery systems could begin to move the world in a safer direction, towards the virtual elimination of these existence-threatening weapons. The nuclear threat has always tended to disappear into an obscure corner of the consciousness of humankind except in brief interludes of impending crisis. If this initiative were to begin to take hold and make a difference then an ongoing effort would be required to keep it on the table in diplomacy and to encourage sustained media attention.

The non-proliferation treaty may still be useful. But it now appears likely that any nation that believes it must have a nuclear weapon to guarantee its security will set out to build one whether it is a signatory to the treaty or not. Even if it signed the treaty, it can argue that it did not surrender its sovereign right to protect itself. It may feel endangered. It may no longer believe it will be protected by others. By taking the initiative to systematically reduce its own stockpiles the United States would take the edge off the blatantly obvious but more or less unmentionable contradiction between its own massive nuclear weaponry and its obsession that Iran, a sovereign state surrounded by potentially hostile nuclear powers, should not be allowed to acquire a single bomb.

The United States could take other initiatives similar to its efforts to avoid nuclear war. It could face up to other looming shadows of catastrophe and look for ways to help humankind slide past the worst. Among the more obvious of these challenges are climate change, cyber conflict, conventional armaments, and global public health.

From where we stand today nothing could seem more difficult to achieve than a firmly established planetary peace which would benefit all of humankind. It seems so far beyond the reach of the possible that we may as well throw up our hands and find something else to think about. What I propose is on the right track, but I'm in no way optimistic. As a Ph.D. in Modern European History and an historian of the coming of the First World War, I know that even with the best of intentions, even when the world seems to be moving in positive directions, even when there are many civilized and competent people in high places, it can suddenly blow apart, sliding from one bloody catastrophe into another.

The virtues which are most important in avoiding catastrophe and pursuing this seemingly impossible dream of a viable and humane world

    SLIDING PAST THE SHADOWS OF CATASTROPHE

peace are persistence, patience, a commitment to nonviolence, and resistance to hawkish hot-heads of all kinds, a willingness to listen and to
compromise, and a relentless consistency in approach. In its simplicity
and because of its simplicity the Global Project offers a comprehensible
pathway for pursuing this seemingly impossible dream.

Chapter 13

Recovering Our Society

Beneath it all we Americans know who we are or, at least, who we want to be: free standing individuals in a society which, as fantastically diverse as it may be, accepts our differences, respects our concerns, wants us to flourish, and is devoted to tough minded values and a democratic political system which is intended to help make this happen and to which we can give our loyal support. This self-understanding of our American identity, these common American aspirations, if not lost, are being successfully undermined by lies and liars, by demagoguery, by partisan sycophants, by exploiters of public ignorance, by purchasers of favors, by the hypocrisies rolled into each of these, and by perennial failures to adequately address pressing social and material challenges.

I have argued that we must recover our politics and our global leadership. To be successful in these critical initiatives, we must, at the same time, strengthen the social and cultural foundations upon which they both depend. To do this, the morality, of mind, imagination, and engagement is the place to start. Then, in determining exactly what is to be done, the overarching goals of realizing the meaning of the common and of minimizing waste come into play.

THE MORALITY

The morality of honesty, of truth-seeking, of respecting the verifiable facts is the most fundamental and imperative of social and cultural challenges. We cannot recover our politics or our leadership without meeting this head on. More Americans believe in nonsense unsupported by the facts than in any other developed country. Of course, these people have the right to believe whatever they wish and the right to say whatever they want to say. They are free to lie profusely, except in court. They may learn to read and write, acquire marketable skills, and navigate successfully in the digital world, and still live in life-worlds fearfully stuffed with lies, irrational beliefs, fake news, conspiracy theories, racism, and demonized opponents.

Nothing is more critical than to win the fight against the culture of dishonesty, against the lies and liars, the self-satisfied ignorance, and the cynical manipulations which are its essentials. This is not in itself a legal battle. It is not an assault on the right to be wrong. But it is a battle for truth-seeking grounded in the evidence, and for an imaginative and empathetic effort to understand others and their life worlds. It must be waged in homes, schools, and the public forum. There will always be lies and liars, but they must not be left in charge. If the United States is to lead by example, if it is to successfully appeal to others, then the culture of dishonesty, which invites distrust, must be disarmed. Who will want to emulate the land of lies and liars?

The morality of the imagination must also be put to work. Even if we feel well protected in our present situations, we Americans must make an imaginative and empathetic effort to understand others and their life-worlds. Many Americans have been doing this, but we must fight against the xenophobic closing of our minds which is growing and is carrying racist messages within it.

Social Capital

Americans do not know each other, not well enough. They tend to know only those inside their own enclaves: economic, political, religious, cultural, ethnic, racial, etc.; and the people beyond these enclaves are often perceived as outsiders, hardly worth knowing, and not to be trusted. This is a great divide in America's social capital, in those personal relationships and institutional affiliations which draw people together. This split is not complete, but it demands attention. It's a social illness which must be treated. Crisis situations, hurricanes, tornados, terrorist attacks, bring out the best in the American people, in all who help the victims, in all those who take personal risks to help them. These manifestations of social capital have a powerful therapeutic value; but they don't seem to solve the underlying problems of social distance. Those need to be addressed.

Particular lines of attack on the weakening of social capital and on the culture of dishonesty need imaginative development requiring an investigative spirit and a willingness to experiment with the most promising options. I imagine reforms in our politics could open the way to policy decisions which would aim at building social capitol and which would be guided at least in part by the goals of realizing the meaning of the common and minimizing waste, particularly the wastage of individuals threatened of being cut of and left behind. For instance, a national service program might be devised as a way to bring virtually all young Americans together across all the dividing lines.

Sources of Support

Though shaky, the foundations are in place for undercutting the culture of dishonesty, for reducing its pernicious role. Millions of parents

          SLIDING PAST THE SHADOWS OF CATASTROPHE

teach their children the importance of truth telling based on fact, the immoral and self-destructive nature of lying, the need for kindness and caring. Millions of teachers echo these values. The parents and teachers of the Parkland High School kids must have been exemplifying these values because their children displayed them in the aftermath of the massacre of their classmates with unprecedented eloquence and courage.

These values are reflected in the work of those journalists who uphold the highest standards of their profession, of those scientists, scholars, and others who are engaged in truth seeking disciplines committed to self-corrective practices. And, of course, there are honorable people everywhere who are turned off by lies and liars and who are, as they understand it, seeking truth and understanding. The foundations are there. But the battle against the culture of dishonesty requires consciously developed collaborative efforts. Parents, teachers, journalists, scientists, scholars and other like-minded people need to band together to create an organized activist resistance. If the political party of reform, suggested above, were to emerge it would necessarily represent this cause.

FREEDOM, TRUTH, AND DEMOCRACY

As the Executive Director of a State Humanities Council, I acquired considerable experience in conceptualizing and implementing public programs in the humanities and the arts. From that experience I can imagine a national public program focused on the respect for truth as freedom's strongest defense and as the cornerstone of a flourishing democracy This program might be called "Freedom, Truth, and Democracy" or be given a more-catchy name. It would depend on the creative imaginations of those who would propose programs designed to reach particular audiences. Among unlimited options, these proposals could be for town halls, radio or television programs, public lectures, reading circles, classroom materials, contests for short stories, poems, or one act plays. These could be deployed through the state humanities and arts councils which reach into every corner of their states, are well known, are generally well respected, and have relevant experience and expertise. To have a national impact, this program would require sustained support from individuals and from public and private organizations and institutions.

Truth-seeking would be promoted broadly with the implication that it is a healthy aspiration within every lifeworld. It would assert the fact that we owe our civilization to an infinite variety of truth seekers, of whom many of the most significant contributors have faced devastating obstacles, sometimes martyrdom, often deadlier enemies than that phalanx of lies, liars, and conspiracy theorists which is undermining truth-seeking in the United States today.

This program would be carried by individuals for whom truth-seeking is central to their work, by scientists, scholars, journalists, jurists, writers, artists, researchers of various kinds, who have earned respect for competence, integrity, and devotion to the search for truth. They would participate in the program in various ways. They would discuss the challenges of truth-seeking in their fields, what it demands, how successful it may be, and where it may fall short; and/or they would talk about themselves, about what brought them to their line of work, how it has shaped who and what they are, and what they expect to do with it in the future. They could consider the relationship of their work to the project's long-term goals

Other resources could be drawn on: the biographies of historically significant truth seekers, of individuals who contributed to scientific understanding; of authors, playwrights, and poets who expressed enduring interpretations of their life-worlds; of historians who from their particular perspectives made sense out of a complex and ambiguous past; of founders and interpreters of religions; and of philosophers who created commanding systems of ideas. The builders of America's constitutional order were truth seekers. Taking what they understood from historical experience and from the failures of the Articles of Confederation to unify relationships, they struggled to create out of their knowledge of history a lasting and workable system of government which would avoid the tyrannies they feared.

EDUCATION

In the United States, we are trying to prepare the young for the world we know, but we are not preparing them for a world we cannot clearly see, but which will surely confront them with many worrisome challenges which could change virtually everything for them. Projections of future employment opportunities dominate our calculations and theirs. This may be a short-term necessity for the markets and for the young who are trying to make realistic career choices; but we are leaving too much out. We must also prepare them to cope with change, wisely and constructively; with the possibilities, for instance, that certain vocational choices which appeal to them today may lead them into dead ends; and that their lifestyle expectations may be radically altered by historical events. Above all else, if we are to rebuild a healthy and dynamic American democracy, we must prepare them for civic engagement which is patriotic, insightful, unselfish, knowledgeable, and accurately informed.

Curricula which are recognizably supportive of the morality of mind, imagination, and engagement must be put in place to help the young understand who they are and where they come from and to discover constructive outlets for their talents, curricula which must be rich in the sciences, social sciences, the humanities, and the arts. These curricula must reach beyond the narrowing confines of a particular society and culture by opening up young minds and imaginations to an empathetic understanding of others with whom they share the planet earth, however different they may seem. These curricula must be open to the creativity of the teachers who teach them to fit the understandings and potentialities of the young.

Education at its best in not only caring but tough minded. It is a civilizing process in which sweetness and light are not always effective. It requires at times, figuratively speaking, a heavy hand. The curricula and its teaching must have a hard edge in the sense that the older children must not be shielded from the dangerous, worrisome challenges of the 21st Century. They must be led to understand that these must be faced up to and that the project's overarching goals offer useful guidelines for confronting them. They must be encouraged to see themselves not as passive victims, but as active shapers of the future.

ECONOMIC REFORM

The morality of mind, imagination and engagement and the project's overarching goals imply that our American economy belongs to the American people, that it is literally "Of the People, by the People, and for the People" and that otherwise it may perish from this earth, smothered under the shadows of catastrophe. This most unpleasant prospect demands thoughtful critiques of the negative impacts that the capitalist economy is having on the United States and the wider world today, explorations of the barriers it raises against what must be done if the United States is to effectively face up to the worrisome challenges of the 21st Century and to realize its potential to help lead humankind to a better place. If required, there should be ample creative room to develop fresh economic arrangements which would, it may be imagined, make constructive use of the powers of the digital revolution and would avoid tyrannical outcomes. No one should want a catastrophic reversion to the failed communist and socialist experiments of the 20th Century.

Global capitalism pursues economic growth as its perpetual motion machine, as a secular Holy Grail. Unfortunately, global capitalism, in spite of its success, presents systemic risks for the American people and all of humankind. Market driven growth threatens to push beyond necessary restraints if a livable planet is to be sustained, if it hasn't already done so in its delayed responses to climate change. Its historical patterns of boom and bust; its emphasis on unrestrained competition, contradicted by its monopolistic practices; its complacent acceptance of creative destruction; its push to privatize the public domain, all must be assessed and dealt with from the perspectives of the global project.

The explosion of economic inequality is a complex systemic development and a looming shadow of catastrophe. Although it is true that the proportion of people living in abject poverty has been much reduced, outsized concentrations of private wealth, supported by oligarchic power, too often expressed in flagrantly luxurious life styles, inevitably produce festering perceptions of material inequality among people who are not necessarily poverty stricken themselves but are in a position to rebel against this perceived injustice. These people may rise up against a social order which seems to be dismissing them as servants of an economy which they perceive as ruthlessly unfair. Making it fairer implies a rebalancing of economic power and more broadly acceptable distributions of income and of asset ownership. These transformational changes would require a lengthy political and legal struggle. They would call for serious attention from the Party of Reform.

Once its dangerous flaws are acknowledged and soberly assessed it is not productive to demonize the capitalist system or all those talented, dedicated, people who are making this hugely complicated and widely beneficial system function with considerable success. But the worrisome challenges and systemic problems demand supervision by a firm hand, by rational governance, a necessity which will always be resisted by those who believe, with little proof, that the system always flourishes best when government stays out of the way.

Public/private Collaboration

In fact, capitalism's success has historically depended on public/private collaborations. This is notably true in the economic history of the United States. Both in opening up economic opportunities and in addressing serious problems, government participation has been essential. It has initiated and collaborated in great infrastructure projects. It has organized the country for war. It has bailed out the capitalist system more than once from its self-destructive episodes and it may have to bail it out again, and more than once. We do not want to emulate the Chinese system, but once the Chinese ruling party decided on a top down government-directed partnership with capitalism it initiated a most spectacular process of economic development.

Private capitalism did not save itself from the ravages of the Great Recession. It was saved by the good fortune of having in place governmental institutions with creative leadership. When the crisis hit, a huge volume of intangible financial resources went up in smoke. Hundreds of billions of dollars evaporated overnight as the markets collapsed. Then the economy was slowly, carefully, and thankfully brought back to health mostly by the Federal Reserve which through rock bottom interest rates and quantitative easing gradually replaced those assets which the crisis poofed away and did so without stimulating inflation. It replenished the coffers of the banks and of individual investors through the economic activity it underwrote. This recovery was government funded; top down Keynesianism skillfully managed. Of course, the Fed's books ballooned, but this did not inflate the economy. Inflation remained incredibly low. The benefits mostly flowed to the very rich, while more bottom up Keynesianism, skillfully managed, would have reduced unemployment, would likely have speeded the recovery, and could have begun to fund a transformational attack on deteriorating and outdated infrastructure.

The economic imperative requires a respect for experts, for professional economists, for all those who process mountains of data seeking understanding of how the economy functions and insights into what might be done to make it function better. Nevertheless, their work may rest on assumptions which are much too narrow and, through complex digital applications, they may reach conclusions which are only tenuously connected to the real, ever-changing world, and to the well-rounded needs of individual human beings.

The moral imperative requires respect for well-qualified experts of all sorts, but it does not require the imprisonment of mind and imagination within the parameters of their expertise. The disciplines of the experts evolve. The moral imperative does not compete with them on their own ground. It is not in itself an expertise, but an approach for coping with unpredictable events and for determining what is to be done in present circumstances in support of two overarching long-term goals.

Standard labels in politics and economics are useful and necessary tools for our more general processes of communication. How could we do without conservative, liberal, right wing, left wing, progressive, reactionary, capitalist, fascist, socialist, communist, and an extended list of other identifying terms. Behind each lies a complicated universe of facts, principles, and influential personalities which need to be considered in an open search for truth. These labels may be passionately defended or employed as jumping off points for passionate attacks. They are often used in ways which are more ambiguous and confusing than enlightening. Whenever possible, they are best avoided in the search for policy solutions tied clearly and precisely to the evidence.

At this time, the word "socialism" is being used mostly for attacks which fail to acknowledge what the term now usually means in discussions of public policy. "Socialism" in most contemporary discourse rejects its 19th and 20th century meaning, which mandated the public ownership of the instruments of production, the factories, the railroads, the mines, the banks, etc. To simplify, the word now mainly stands for the idea of putting the well-being of people ahead of the amassing of private wealth. This controversial principle is consistent with the Global Project's overarching goals which prioritize the well-being of humankind. But once that is said, exactly what this means, and the economic arrangements which it implies, must be thought through in the decades ahead. At the heart of the problem, discussed above in Chapter 2, is the age-old issue of who owns what and why. In the 21st Century this issue must not be characterized, as some would have it, as a simple binary conflict between greedy selfishness and humanitarian generosity. Philosophically and practically, it is infinitely more complicated than that. But it remains an issue which cannot be avoided.

"Public Works" may seem to have an affinity to the original meaning of "socialism", that is, of government ownership and control of the means of production, but in the United States the term has generally referred to government initiated infrastructure projects which may be nothing bigger than a local sewage system; or they may be huge undertakings like the interstate highway system, a public works project of the Eisenhower administration, which helped sustain the decades long expansions of industry and commerce and to profoundly influence the ways Americans live their lives. The New Deal's Tennessee Valley Authority (TVA), a massive public project, provided the electricity for the World War II Manhattan Project which gave the United States the atomic bomb. Setting aside the necessities of defense, "the military industrial complex", which President Eisenhower saw as a rising danger to the Republic, should be recognized for what it is, a massive public investment loaded with infrastructure projects.

I conclude this essay with these outstanding examples of government initiated public works because the United States is long overdue to develop new ambitious projects and give them top priority. It needs to do this to meet the challenges of the 21ˢᵗ Century both domestically and in its international posture. But the challenges seem almost insurmountable. Action seems unlikely because the needs are so immense and because of political paralysis and hostility to big government. Much of the country's infrastructure, inherited from the past, is crumbling and needs large public investments. There are other new demands imposed by 21ˢᵗ Century realities. Most obvious is climate change which requires a complex menu of public projects in response to its various impacts. Many problems cannot be resolved except by democratic governance of the highest quality. Public/private partnerships wherever possible; otherwise government funded and managed public works.

The Party of Reform could take on an invaluable catalytic role. It could encourage a thorough investigation of national structural needs, and encourage political debate on how national resources could best be allocated to meet them. To effectively manage these initiatives, it might suggest new congressional committees to draft and oversee the legislation, and a new cabinet department responsible for its implementation.

Conclusion to Part II

The Global Project, presented in Part I, provided the intellectual foundations for the discussions in Part II of what we Americans must do to bring about the recovery of our country, to look ahead and confront the existential challenges of the 21st Century. In each Part, the morality of mind, imagination, and engagement, and the overarching goals of realizing the meaning of the common and minimizing of waste offer a place to start for deciding what to do.

If the United States is to face up to all the worrisome challenges of the 21st Century, if it is to offer the world the leadership it desperately needs, it must introduce whatever structural reforms in its political culture are necessary to reestablish the legitimacy and effectiveness of its democratic institutions. It must transform its system of education away from its narrow emphasis on vocational preparation to a broader and more inclusive emphasis on preparing the young to deal wisely and effectively with their civic responsibilities and with a world changing rapidly in dangerous and unpredictable ways. It must subordinate its economic system to long term considerations and reshape it in the direction of the overarching goals. It must take the lead in wringing chauvinism out of national identities, beginning with its own, in overcoming sovereign jealousies, and in endowing international institutions with sufficient sovereignty to effectively cope with global challenges.

If the United States is to respond successfully to these imperatives then the struggle against lies, liars, conspiracy theorists, fake news, and demagoguery must be won. No total victory is possible; but their poisonous grip on the minds and imaginations of far too many Americans must be loosened. The morality of mind, imagination and engagement offers a powerful antidote, particularly in so far as it is successfully integrated into the education of the young.

Author's Postscript

In my preface I indicated my need to reconcile my two identities, as a citizen of a globalizing world and as a patriotic American, identities which superficially appear to be at odds. I was asking myself how to pull these identities together into a coherent and consistent whole. My essay represents my attempt to do that.

As an historian I knew that trying to predict the future against all that is unknown is mostly a futile exercise. But I also recognized that in this 21st Century we have yet to successfully face up to a growing cluster of threats to the human prospect. We have yet to clearly confront them and to find ways to evade or prevent them. I understood that there are many reasons for this, but I also saw that among the most obvious is short term thinking, the widespread imprisonment of minds and imaginations in the comforting immediacies of the present.

I also assumed and firmly believed that successful responses to these threats would have to depend on honest truth-seeking, that the challenges to humankind would never be resolved by lies, liars, and purveyors of conspiracy. So it seemed to me that the best I could do would be to lay aside most of my personal opinions on policy (of which I have many), but which I have no reason to believe are necessarily better than those of others, and look for a place to begin, for a place where I could begin in the reconciliation of my identities, for a starting place which might appeal to other human beings both globally and locally whatever their life-worlds, which might even offer a universal approach to the challenges confronting humankind.

I understood that this starting place would be stillborn if it did not offer powerful lines of attack on these challenges, comprehensible guidance for the long struggle amidst ever changing circumstances. It was clear to me that this required long-term goals which could be helpful whether the problems addressed were global, national, or local. It was clear to me that a complex menu of highly specific goals would not work, that the goals must be simple, understandable, aligned with the realities and needs of human nature, and of consistent validity. This led me to posit two overarching goals: the realization of the common, of the constructive commonalities upon which survival may depend; and the minimization of waste, the wastage of a natural world supportive of life and of those multitudes who are threatened with being wasted and discarded.

The Place to Start came down to an invitation to individuals to take self-shaping steps in nurturing their identity, in internalizing their freedom, and in engaging in their life-worlds guided by the morality of truth-seeking and by the universally relevant long-term goals. It offers them a pathway to existential self-development and to a confident and integrated selfhood. For me it offered values and goals applicable to my global and my national concerns and fostered a more or less consistent approach to both.

Sliding Past the Shadows of Catastrophe should not be incorrectly identified as a manifesto. The typical manifesto is the work of a dogmatic crank who has all the answers to whatever disturbs him. My essay is not about answers. It is about an approach. It is not dogmatic. It depends on Socratic ignorance. It invites research and investigation and problem-solving dialogue. Its identification of the looming shadows of catastrophe is open ended. They are shadows because it's impossible to precisely weigh them or predict their ultimate impacts even though much about them is now known. The great drivers of 21st Century change must be managed but no detailed formulas are offered as to how this is to be done. The United States has been drifting deeper into partisan paralysis and corruption. It is passing through a disastrous presidency. Fundamental institutions are being undermined. It must get its house in order if it is to do its part in leading humankind to a better place. It may not be able to do that without the interventions of a powerful movement towards reform.

Those who like myself go on living comfortably in the developed world and are better situated than most of humankind to work towards the project's goals should be asking ourselves where we stand in regard to this global responsibility. Aside from my attempt to think through my understanding of what must be done, I'm not doing much myself. Instead, I mostly go on living in a pleasant well-insulated life-world.

As an aging white man, I've been exceptionally fortunate: brought up in a loving family, given all the educational advantages, enabled in my vocational choices to march to the beat of my own drummer, and now happily retired in the Michigan countryside with my wife of over sixty years with whom I participate in the unfolding stories of our children and grandchildren. Those who, like myself, are among the more privileged members of the American middle class and who consider themselves committed to values and goals which are similar to mine should recognize the existential hypocrisy built into our life-worlds, about how the way we live works at cross purposes with the minimization

                SLIDING PAST THE SHADOWS OF CATASTROPHE

of waste and the realization of the common and diverts our attention from the looming shadows of catastrophe. I do not like to think of myself as a hypocrite, but I am deeply immersed, as are multitudes of others, in this existential hypocrisy.

My wife and I could qualify as poster-children. Our old rambling country house requires obscene quantities of propane to keep us warm in winter. To offset this, we could be burning cords of firewood in our fireplaces. Our old apple trees keep shedding branches which I collect and burn off at the back of our property. Only two of us are now living in our big old family home, but we still generate enough trash, mostly discarded packaging, to fill a large wheeled container almost every week. My wife's 1982 Mercedes diesel emits clouds of black exhaust. We are living comfortably in a life-world which helps to make things worse. That's what I mean by existential hypocrisy. And, of course, we are not alone. Far from it.

We try to do better. The ancient Mercedes seldom leaves the garage. We try to remember to turn off the lights. We do not load our acre and half of lawn with fertilizers the way we once did. We've moved our newspaper subscriptions from paper to on line, and we write modest checks to causes which appear to be working in the direction of the global common and/or towards the minimization of waste. This all helps a little to edge the world towards a more viable future, but if the goals of the 21st Century Project are to be reached these are microscopic pittances. The remedy to this existential hypocrisy depends on yet to be determined transformations in our human life-worlds. We know that much is to be done; we can help a little; but these transformations, if they are to be brought about creatively, wisely, and peacefully will take time; and they must be global and they must include all of humankind.

We existential hypocrites, however comfortable our life-worlds, are caught along with all of humankind in a huge existential trap. We are trapped in an economic, technological, political, and cultural global life-world which is moving with overpowering momentum in dangerous and unsustainable directions, which is mostly indifferent or oblivious to the looming shadows of catastrophe and which blocks the way to timely evasions. The Place to Start offers humankind a gateway through which to escape this existential trap, an escape which begins in people across the world who sincerely look for truth and make an honest effort to understand their own life-worlds and the life-worlds of others, who are builders of community, not destroyers, and who are doing what they can to protect the underpinnings of life.

NOTES

Note #1, p.8 Truth-seeking, as it is be understood in this essay, is existentially critical to the fate of humankind, not only for survival but to light pathways towards a common realization of shared identity. It is not my intent, however, to dismiss philosophical and cosmological investigations into the nature of "truth" which may conclude that there is no such thing as "the truth" or that, if there is, it is hiding beyond the reach of our intellectual capacities and/or of our technologies. Paradoxically, for the serious truth-seeker these arguments deserve consideration and respect, but they do not undercut the existential necessity of truth-seeking as it is presented in this essay.

Note #2, p.58 For me and I imagine for others the election of Donald Trump was not particularly surprising. In my novel, *On the Way to a Coup D'Etat, Xlibris 2012*, I present a President, James Millwright, who exemplifies the values at the center of *Sliding Past the Shadows of Catastrophe*. Viciously attacked, he devotes his political and managerial skills to move the country in more promising directions. After he fails at most of what he tried to do, I follow the downward drift of his successors, whom I call "the Mediocrities". These include a self-promoting real estate mogul and end with a larger than life demagogic hip hop artist, whom I call "The MAN", who fills stadiums for his powerful rants with adoring fans, with devoted followers who respond at the climax of his diatribes by firing their handguns into the air in earth-shaking explosions of support. In the end, as a last resort, the Man is removed from office by young military officers in a patriotically driven Coup d'Etat. This addition to the Preamble of the United States Constitution is an example of what these conspirators try to do to bring about a national renewal.

Note #3, p.66 This is drawn from *On the Way to a Coup D'Etat,* from the story of national renewal. See Note #2

Note #4, p.44 The admonitions below are also from *On the Way to a Coup D'Etat.* They are drawn from an address presented by the President's wife, Ann Millwright, to the organizers of an international association of master teachers dedicated to a global revolution in education.